# Baking

### with passion

Baker & Spice

# Baking

## with passion

exceptional recipes for real breads, cakes and pastries

Dan Lepard and Richard Whittington

special photography by Peter Williams

Quadrille

to Karen Copland and Barry Stephens

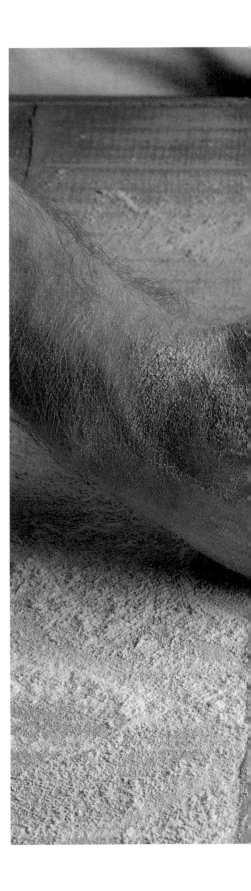

Art Director: Mary Evans
Publishing Director: Anne Furniss
Project Editor: Norma MacMillan
Design: Paul Welti
Food for photography: Dan Lepard (breads),
    Jane Suthering (cakes and pastries)
Stylist: Róisín Nield
Production: Vincent Smith, Julie Hadingham

First published in 1999 by Quadrille Publishing Limited,
Alhambra House, 27–31 Charing Cross Road,
London WC2H 0LS

This paperback edition first published in 2000
Reprinted in 2003, 2005, 2006

Cataloguing in Publication Data: a catalogue record for this book
is available from the British Library

ISBN-13: 978 184400 034 0
ISBN-10: 1 84400 034 6

Printed and bound in China

# Contents

# Introducing Baker & Spice

"I think bread is special, something simple and honest yet delicious. Every time you break it, smell it, eat it, it makes life a little better, even if it is only for 5 minutes. Good bread is something you never get bored with. It delights afresh, every day. In essence, it describes both who we are at Baker & Spice and why we are." GAIL STEPHENS

Baker & Spice was not an idea that sprang fully formed into Gail Stephens' mind. Her most extraordinary and beautiful shop that sits so prettily in smart Walton Street in London started its life as a window for her existing trade-baking business. It was only gradually, as the Victorian ovens were restarted and on-site production began for the local community, that it took shape and flourished, developing the unique identity that has made it famous.

When you visit the shop the first impressions are overwhelming. This is the bakery and pâtissierie of your dreams and those dreams were probably set in Paris, not London. As you admire the stacks of beautiful breads and trays of captivating pastries giving off their sweet, alluring smells – all of them hand-made by bakers working on the premises and using traditional ingredients and methods – it is hard to believe that the roots of such excellence were in vans, not stone ovens, in a delivery service for bread baked by other people, for customers too small for the big bakers to be bothered with. Today's most shining star in British artisanal baking has its roots in an innovative and successful service operation. With its sound business administration providing financial independence, it allowed Gail Stephens to set the shop up in a way that was thought by many to be commercially untenable in today's marketplace.

"The way the shop is run is really based on how we trade," she says, explaining that the raw ingredients define an attitude as well as a style of food. "I have always been concerned about the provenance as well as the quality of the ingredients we work with. I have never bought solely on price and was warned that my ethical concerns would bankrupt me. The irony is that today the business is very successful.

"We are what we buy, and that has moral as well as price consequences. We use as much that is organic as possible. We work with the seasons and are very careful about where our raw materials come from. Does it have to travel half way round the world to get to Walton Street? If something comes from the Third World, who exploited whom to get it here? I don't sit in the office and buy blind on the telephone. I go to Covent Garden four times a week, and read and check every label on every box of fresh produce that I buy. I smell and feel the goods as well as taste them. Once a month I go to a big dried fruit, nut and spice importer. Buying is never on auto-pilot. I really spend a lot of time with suppliers to get it right.

"We bake things that people respond to in a dramatic way because everything we sell is baked on the premises. What you see is what you get and what you get is what we make. And that involves learned technique and very hard work. The whole point of Baker & Spice is that it is self-contained; we don't buy in anything ready-made. We do things the way people used to do them, which in the age of factory farming and the supermarket have largely been forgotten or deliberately ignored. Every day has its own identity. The life span of the product and the way it is produced is just that – a day – and then everything starts from scratch again. Practically, that means seven 18-hour working days in every week.

"Changes occur in what is baked in some sense by natural progression, but also by listening to the customers. Partly because of that we have become a real village shop. We are the neighbourhood. We reflect it and it reflects us."

Baker & Spice is remarkable in its consistent delivery, but this is the direct consequence of the calibre of the staff Gail Stephens has brought together over a three-year period. This is not an anonymous place and the people who work here are encouraged to have an identity as a part of a team whose members inevitably change with time but who share the same commitment to quality achieved in an ethical environment.

This is not like a restaurant where front of house and back of house function autonomously and often with ill-concealed animosity. Here the two are clearly, happily and inextricably intertwined. They work together and you cannot see the join, because the service is a seamless process from the cooking to the customer. Indeed, one of the shop's more unusual aspects is in the direct communication between those who cook at the back with the customers, sometimes even serving them. As freshly baked loaves are brought through or another beautiful cake is displayed, it is discussed and commented on. Regulars travel miles for their morning croissant, often in the summer eating it still warm at one of the small tables on the pavement in front of the shop.

"The achievement of quality in what we sell is only part of the relationship that connects the individual customer to the process at the back of the shop, where what they buy is made," says Karen Copland, the shop manager. "The shop has to work from the front to the back and from the back to the front. It is important that the people who cook the food don't feel separated from the selling of it. They come in and out of the shop, and they talk to the customers. This is how we all feel it should be."

## The bakery

Underneath the street level in Walton Street are two brick ovens, each with the original stone-covered baking floor covering 10 square metres. The ovens were built and installed in 1902 by Robert Hannington and W.H. Young & Co, both Islington-based companies with excellent reputations. Originally fuelled by coal, the steam-generating ovens also provided hot water for the bakery. The steam in a professional oven helps to develop the crust and gives a wonderful bronze colour to the bread.

During the 1950s, the ovens were oil-fired, the fuel being piped from outside tanks to the burners that ran around the circumference of the oven. The smoke and excess steam would be carried through a twisting tunnel to the chimney, where it would escape to make its stinking contribution to the smogs that polluted London's air until the Clean Air Act was introduced in 1957.

When Gail Stephens took over the property from Justin de Blank these ovens were still in use, by then fired by gas. After minor renovations and the addition of a steam-injection system, the ovens were ready to bake bread once again.

Traditionally, breads are put into the oven on heavily floured wooden peels, flat beech-wood heads attached to long shafts. Nobody makes these peels in Britain, so they had to be imported from France. Another investment was a double-sized 'parisienne', a cupboard used

to protect the dough as it rests on unbleached linen sheets. Dozens of cloth-lined reed baskets, in which the big sourdoughs sit during their long fermentation, help to shape the loaves as they prove, and these again had to be sourced from France. For breads requiring a long, chilled rest over many hours, a temperature-controlled retarder-prover that could hold over 200 small loaves was installed.

An Artofex mixer capable of working two sacks of flour at a time was also introduced, a British machine invented to replicate the hand-kneading of doughs in wooden troughs, which was the standard practice in bakeries for hundreds of years. This superior and expensive mixer is popular in France and is today mainly sold there. Its unique configuration helps give the bread an irregular aeration – different sized bubbles of air throughout the crumb – and its gentle slow mixing helps develop the gluten strands.

## The breads

Apparently similar constructions of flour, water and yeast can deliver very different textures and complex, deep flavours. Wheat flours, from the darkest moist wholewheat to cream-coloured, soft milled flour, rye flours, grains of corn, rice and malted wheat kernels are selected from traditional mills in England, France and Ireland for Baker & Spice breads. In all, more than a dozen different types of flour, much of it organic and stoneground, are mixed together in different proportions to create individual bread recipes. The blending of flours is a key to creating the 'wild-yeast' levains and poolishes that raise doughs naturally, and

which contribute significantly to the complex, slightly sour flavour of the finished breads. This is the application of learned practice, essentially artisanal skills which impose consistency on the loaves. There are no chemicals or genetically modified soya improvers to speed things up or make things easier, just the passionate application of knowledge and sheer hard work.

New breads are developed by imagining the finished loaf and then carefully constructing the mix of flours, liquids, leavening materials and techniques. Each bread is created with its own mix of sour starters or fresh active yeast, flours, grains and, in some recipes, fruit and fruit juices, vegetables, nuts, fresh herbs and oils. The sourdoughs are based on four different wild yeast cultures, selected for their proven ability to create healthy, vigorous starters. These vary in moisture content and flour type, and are cared for by regular refreshment and vigorous aeration, activity that in the bakery occurs at programmed intervals throughout each 24-hour period.

The bakery works 18 hours a day, seven days a week, from 10pm until about 7am the next morning and then from 10am until 6 or 7pm. As many of the processes involved in making the breads take days, each baker will have a hand in the production of every single loaf of bread produced. As an example, the Boule de Meule, a traditional French wholemeal sourdough, will have been mixed early one morning, developed and shaped during the day, rested for 12 hours and finally baked very early the next day.

The skills that each member of the baking team brings to the process are capable of wider application since, unusually for a professional baker in Britain, many of the breads are made in small batches, as are the cakes and pastries. So the techniques used and the amount of what is being produced are on a scale closer to domestic cooking than is typical.

## The cakes

There is a tradition of thoughtful cake making – the skilful mixing of fine ingredients in a bowl, combined by hand and baked in small batches – which has found continued professional expression at Baker & Spice. It is honest food representing the very best home baking from around the world.

Mass-produced cakes tend to be very basic, but are dressed up after they are baked to make them look more special than they really are. This is quite the opposite of the Baker & Spice approach, where there is little or no decoration of the cakes after they cool from the oven. Here everything is in the making. Thus the final flavour in every Bramley apple and Calvados cake is achieved before the cakes are baked. There is no icing to camouflage and no decoration to distract from poor texture and flavour. What is achieved is the result of the best ingredients and careful baking techniques, nothing more and nothing less.

## The pastries and brioches

'*Viennoiserie*' describes the highly specialised area of croissant and puff pastry making, something in which Baker & Spice excels. Patrick Lozach was the man who first created the croissants, the brioche and fine butter pastries for the shop. Trained in Brittany over 20 years ago, his work reflects the traditions of 'old school' French baking, before the additives and colours of the chemical industry took hold of the small pâtisseries. As with the bread at Baker & Spice, the source of the ingredients for the *Viennoiserie* plays an important part in the quality Patrick was able to achieve. The doughs are mixed using French 'T550', a slow-milled low-extraction wheat flour that gives a crisp texture to the exterior of the croissants and to baguettes. The flour's low gluten content holds the layers intact and separate, through repeated turning and folding, creating a tender melting crumb and a crisp short finish to the crust.

Much of the cheaper *Viennoiserie* sold in Britain, and increasingly in France, contains an orange-dyed butter, a mixture of milk fat from EC countries, reprocessed and packaged as 'French butter'. The croissants at Baker & Spice are made exclusively with L'Escure, an *appellation controllé* unsalted French butter. L'Escure is not used because it is from France, but because it is the best butter there is. The pain au chocolat is filled with Belgian Callibaut Couverture – a fine high-cocoa-content chocolate with a strong bittersweet taste. The almond croissants are filled with ground almonds, sugar, butter and egg yolks. No artificial flavours, no essences, no bulking agents, just lots of almonds and fresh butter.

*Baking with passion* encapsulates all the skills of the bakers at Baker & Spice in recipes which, while detailed, communicate simply and logically how to get the best results. Everything is explained, from the consequences of using different yeasts to the impact of working with different flours. You will learn how to replicate the steam-injection used in the bakery to achieve crusted loaves with a delightful chewy crumb. You will discover that working with wetter doughs delivers better bread, and that techniques for gentle kneading and turning improve aeration and texture. All the recipes have been tested in a domestic kitchen using non-professional electric and gas ovens.

Everything that is done in the bakery to maximise the efficiency of production carries through usefully into the practice of the domestic baker. Whether creating tangy sourdough breads with wild yeast starters or learning how to layer pastry with air and butter to produce beautifully crisp and light mille feuilles, this is the most practical of kitchen handbooks. It is not about the hard work of a professional baker, but a story of finding and giving pleasure through the making of delicious things for everyday enjoyment at home.

# Essentials

Breadmaking has traditionally been a separate activity within bakeries that also produce cakes, pastries and biscuits, demanding very different skills and time frames. This is the case at Baker & Spice, where different teams work in each area. But the bringing together in the shop of everything that is made expresses the totality of baking as a specialised cooking discipline and, in the range of techniques, tastes and textures on display, a happy reflection of the home baking experience. If bread is the staff of life, then cakes, pastries and biscuits are part of baking's pleasure principle.

# OUR DAILY BREAD

Good bread is a beautiful thing. It is a joy to look at and always a pleasure to eat. Good bread never cloys and we never grow bored with it. Bread is as honest and basic as it is emblematic and significant. Just as rice symbolises life in the East and no meal is considered complete without it, so bread is at the very heart of Western civilisation. Give us this day our daily bread.

The smell of freshly baked bread, its crackling-crisp crust, its texture when it is broken or sliced and the consistency of its interior crumb, make it an immensely satisfying and complex culinary assembly. Yet its constituent parts are no more than flour, water and yeast tempered with a small amount of salt. As you bite into a piece of good baguette you experience all these elements in a taste that combines an underlying sweetness from the wheat, an almost imperceptible balancing sourness from the yeast and a stronger, contrasting slightly bitter note from the caramelised

crust, the whole drawn together and given depth by the salt.

A sourdough brings different and much stronger flavours, its defining characteristic the acid tang that comes from its lengthy, natural leavening with wild yeasts, the texture altogether denser, more robust and substantial. This is the darker-coloured country bread of ancient tradition, moister, more chewy and longer lasting, a description that in contemporary usage implies chemical additives but here means the product of its entirely natural development. Such rustic loaves were originally baked in 4 kilo ovals, family bread to last a week, changing in taste and texture with progressive cutting and ageing, yet taking days before staling. Even when too tough to chew, it may be eaten in soups or crumbed to add texture or to thicken a variety of dishes. This is indeed bread as the staff of life.

Baking great bread does have a kind of alchemy, for in its artisanal production there are always elements that are beyond technique, though not beyond technical comprehension. Ambient factors play important roles but are not beyond the wit of any competent cook to understand and harness. Even when the same recipe is used, the resulting bread will vary from place to place as different flours, the water used, temperature, humidity and even air pressure impact in different ways. Individual technique also plays a part, all these things contributing to the unique quality of the finished loaf.

Excellent bread is not only baked by master bakers. It can be made successfully at home and in standard domestic ovens. The specialist's oven frequently incorporates controllable steam injection and it is this steam that helps to form a perfect crust while preventing that crust from being impossibly hard. Most of the breads that we tend to regard as the exclusive preserve of the professional, such as baguettes and sourdoughs, or loaves baked in direct contact with the stone floor of a cavernous bread oven, can in fact be produced in any oven capable of high heat and using a baking stone, steam being generated by spraying water from a bottle.

As with any area of cooking expertise, great bakers have a vocation, and part of it is the ability to communicate how to achieve good and consistent results and to help others find pleasure in the processes of bread's creation. This book is about how to bake good bread at home. With practice, it can become great bread that changes the quality of any and every meal for the better.

# FLOUR

Without good flour there can be no good bread. Skill alone cannot achieve it. Flour may be defined as the finely ground meal of any edible grain, though a reasonable assumption today is that it will probably be made from wheat, a description of such vast generalisation, perhaps it obscures more than it clarifies. What makes one flour good or appropriate for a given task may make it unsuitable for another. A bag of soft self-raising flour, with chemical improvers and raising agents, is unquestionably a white wheat flour, but it is not the stuff from which a good loaf can be made. It may, however, conversely and perversely, be used to bake a decent cake and perhaps a reasonable soda bread.

The history of baking is at least 6000 years old, though what was called bread at different periods during that time has varied hugely from the earliest coarse-textured flat cakes cooked on a griddle over an open fire to the airy complexity of today's perfect baguette baked in a steam-injected oven. Wheat is capable of being ground more finely than most other grains, a fact that has always been identified with privilege. The bread of the poor for thousands of years was grim coarse stuff of millet, oats, barley and rye, perceived by those with higher standards of living as a damning card of social identity. In hard times virtually anything might bulk the breads of poverty, including pulses, chestnuts, vetches, weeds and – when starvation loomed – sawdust and even clay.

As the superiority of wheat over other grains reflected social hierarchies, so its finest expression was seen to be an ever more refined flour with less and less husk and wheat germ left in. The whiter and finer the bread, the higher up the social ladder the eater was perceived to be. It is only in the last 100 years that the beneficial role the bits sifted out and discarded to achieve this cosmetic enhancement might play in diet and digestion has been recognised, leading to today's rapidly expanding market for breads that add value by deliberately including bran from the husk, nutty-tasting wheat germ and other grains and seeds. From a nutritional point of view, such 'wholemeal' loaves are not intrinsically better for you, unless your diet is completely deficient in B vitamins and fibre. Choice today between white or brown, chewy or finely textured, is really only a matter of taste.

A typical grain of wheat is about 5–6mm long and 3mm thick. It is made up of a multi-layered cellulose husk – the bran – which surrounds a hard centre, 20 per cent of which is the oily and vitamin-rich wheat germ – the embryo from which it germinates – the rest being the starchy endosperm. This contains all the gluten-forming proteins that the embryo consumes as it starts to grow. Millers begin by selecting and buying a number of different wheat varieties to create

a mix that they can reproduce
consistently. Infrared analysis determines
key characteristics, including protein
content and humidity levels. Cleaning
involves brushing and the use of magnets
to remove metal contamination prior to
washing and drying before milling.

Since industrial roller technology was
first developed in the 1830s by the Swiss,
most flours have been steel-ground, a high-
speed process that generates heat from
friction and that damages various aspects of
the flour, including the gluten level and the
vitamins and enzymes found in the wheat
germ. Roller milling passes cleaned wheat
grains between a succession of ribbed steel
rollers rotating at high speed in opposite
directions, the bran and germ being
separated and sifted out, leaving behind
only the whiter flour derived from the
endosperm. This is ground finer and finer
with progressive sifting between each
grinding – known technically as bolting –

until an ivory-coloured and powdery flour results. The extraction of the oily wheat germ means the flour keeps better, but the flavour is less pronounced. Once milled and stored, flour bleaches naturally with time, but storing is expensive so this whitening is now usually achieved rapidly with chlorine gas, after which the flour may have tiny amounts of niacin, riboflavin, thiamin and iron added to compensate for the vitamins and minerals lost during steel grinding.

The ancient practice of grinding wheat between slowly turning stones, which has gone on uninterrupted for thousands of years – at first powered by hand, later by water mills and today by electricity – is once again becoming more common. As a more discerning market continues to develop, so higher quality stoneground flours, once only available to the baking trade or at retail through healthfood shops, are to be found in better supermarkets. Yet this remains a fledgling business when compared to France where some 2500 independent small mills operate – in Britain there are perhaps 25. The most significant difference between French and British flours is that the former are milled at a slower speed, resulting in flours that retain more of the wheat's gluten. British bakers tend to achieve higher gluten flours for breadmaking by adding harder imported Canadian flours to the bulk of home-grown flours, an expensive practice because of high import tariffs. The higher the protein level, the less bran the flour will contain.

White flours not described as strong are low in gluten, in other words 'soft'. As a general rule, flours for making bread are harder, the hardest containing as much as 14 per cent of the total weight as gluten-forming proteins. Some breadmaking flours, like the French T550 used for baguettes, are quite soft but have other important qualities, including a low water-absorbing quotient, that make them ideal for this application. Soft flours are mostly used with chemical raising agents in wet batters for making cakes or to make pastries. Flour described as self-raising is soft flour that includes baking powder and other 'improvers'. Improver is the trade name for any chemical added to a flour to accentuate a given characteristic, for example to slow staling or to encourage and accelerate a particular process such as yeast activation. These are the standard tools of industrial baking, but have no valid role to play in the artisanal or home baker's breadmaking.

So-called wholewheat or wholemeal flours are darker in colour because they are made using the whole grain or the endosperm plus some of the wheat germ and husk. The precise percentages determine how dark and strong tasting the flour will be. Wholemeal flours consequently have a nuttier taste, which is imparted by the oily wheat germ. The inclusion of wheat germ and bran affects more than taste and texture, impacting on the gluten action and resulting in a lower rise and a denser loaf.

In this book, we use several different flours, some on their own and others in combination. With French flours the T numeral is a designation describing the degree of sifting from whole grain, from the coarsest wholemeal to the finest white. The T stands for *taux des cendres*, the ash level left behind after a flour has been incinerated in a laboratory at 900°C. The greater the amount of ash, the higher the level of bran in the flour. Thus the T550 of baguette flour indicates that 55mg of ash is left after burning 100g of standard white flour.

## TYPES OF FLOUR USED AT BAKER & SPICE

**T450** a soft, fine French flour which we use for most of our cakes and biscuits. Substitute any ordinary plain flour.
**T550** French white baguette flour; finely ground, soft but with a low moisture absorbency level. You can substitute a mixture of low-gluten plain flour and strong flour – see individual recipes for specific quantities.

**'00' Italian flour** unlike the carefully regulated French T designations, the description of '00' applied to Italian flour is not an absolute description of a protein level. As a general rule it describes a relatively hard flour, typically used for pasta-making and bread baking, but different millers will produce flours of varying degrees of hardness.

**Doves Farm organic strong white flour** a classic stoneground white flour from Hungerford.

**Churchill strong white flour** similar to Doves Farm.

**Odlum's Irish cream flour** a white self-raiser and the best flour we have come across for soda bread and scones. We also use it when making cakes.

**Farine de meule (T850)** a French light wholemeal, pinkish in colour with no discernible flecks of bran.

**Farine de meule (T1100)** 100 per cent wholemeal, this French flour includes all the husk and germ.

**Granary flour** 100 per cent wholemeal with whole malted wheat and barley grains.

**English organic wholemeal flour** 100 per cent of the grain; a strong brown flour.

**Campaillou** developed in France in 1970, it includes malt and dried levain to give a slightly sour flavour; it also includes the yeast catalyst amyl amylase.

**Farine de seigle** a French 100 per cent rye flour, dark and with a strong and distinctive taste; its inclusion in a loaf changes the colour appreciably while the chemical make-up of the rye grain inhibits gluten action in the wheat flour with which it is mixed, producing a denser texture.

# NOTES FOR THE COOK

• For recipes that are raised with active yeast, we always use fresh yeast in the bakery, but in adapting recipes for this book we have opted for fast-action, or easyblend, yeast instead. Fast-action yeast is universally available, completely reliable and absolutely consistent. If you wish to use fresh yeast, simply double the quantity. Thus, a 7g sachet of fast-action yeast is the equivalent of 15g fresh yeast.

• The amount of yeast used changes the rate at which fermentation and consequent rise take place and the texture and keeping quality of a loaf. The less yeast used, the longer a loaf will take to prove. Over-yeasting will speed proving, but will produce a thin crust and bread that stales rapidly.

• The temperature at which you add water to a dough must be determined by the relative temperatures of the other elements involved. Thus, if you keep your flour in a cold place and the bowl of the mixer is cold, you need to compensate by making the water hotter and by warming the mixing bowl. Aim for a dough temperature of 22–24°C. Whether your kitchen is cold or hot will also make a difference.

• Ambient temperature is a key determining feature in yeast activity. While yeasts work at temperatures as low as 3°C, the majority of doughs are raised at temperatures that maximise fermentation. When a very warm environment is called for, the airing cupboard with a typical temperature of 28–30°C is ideal. All other times, a 'warm place' means a temperature around 20–23°C, draught-free. Where specific temperatures are required, this is always spelled out in the recipes.

• All recipes use medium eggs, which can weigh anything from 53g to 63g. We have assumed an average weight of 60g per egg.

• The salt of choice in this book is Maldon, the best flake sea salt in the world. To assist its even distribution throughout the dough, it is good practice to blitz a box full in a food processor to give a uniform, fine grind. This fine salt has, of course, many other uses.

• The use of bottled, still spring water is specified throughout. This does not rule out the use of tap water, but bottled water is less likely to contain chlorine or other chemicals that may impede yeast activity. This is particularly important with wild yeasts which are sensitive to chemicals, even in very low concentrations. Organic ingredients are recommended for the same reason. The less contaminated a water and flour starter environment, the faster and more aggressively the airborne yeasts will culture and work.

• When sufficiently baked any loaf will have lost a lot of moisture. While with experience you can tell by smell, feel and appearance when a loaf is properly cooked, a practical test is to weigh it before it goes in the oven. When you think it is done, weigh it straight from the oven. If ready it should be 20 per cent lighter than when it went in.

# OVENS AND EQUIPMENT

All the recipes in this book have been tested in standard but contemporary gas and electric ovens without convection. Before starting to bake, invest in an oven thermometer and check your oven's maximum temperature. You may be in for an unpleasant surprise. Even brand new and expensive ovens carry no guarantees that they will achieve the 250°C you really need for at least the initial baking of many breads. If your oven is more than a few degrees below this you need to have the problem investigated by an engineer. Usually the cause is a faulty thermostat or that the oven has been wrongly calibrated. If the oven is new, you should have no difficulty in having this rectified. Even if it is out of guarantee, there are companies that repair and maintain ovens, and one of these should be able to help. A more difficult problem to overcome with an under-performing gas cooker is gas pressure. Your gas supplier should be contacted if this turns out to be the cause of an oven not achieving high temperatures. Gas pressure may also drop if the in-house gas distribution is linked to other appliances, such as central heating boilers.

As all keen cooks know, you never seem to have too much cooking equipment and there is always a use for another bowl, whisk or sieve. For baking you must have accurate scales. A powerful table-top electric mixer is another great asset. Strong flours demand strong and lengthy kneading, which is hard work done by hand.

Wherever possible, we have suggested the minimum rather than the maximum requirements. Thus, instead of the wooden peel used by bakers to slide bread into the oven, we suggest using a rimless metal baking sheet. A spray bottle or plant mister will provide you with a steam-generating capability, but be sure to give it a cycle in the dishwasher if it was previously filled with a cleaning product.

**MUST HAVES:**

measuring jugs and spoons

scales (in 5g increments) – digital is best

table-top electric mixer with dough hook, paddle or beater
 and whisk attachments

hand balloon whisks

food processor

selection of mixing bowls in different sizes

plastic containers for levains and poolishes (2 litre with lids)

wooden spoons, numerous

wooden board for shaping

metal dough scraper

plastic and rubber spatulas

palette knife

scissors

rolling pin

rimless metal baking sheet (for peel)

linen cloths and tea towels

oven thermometer

several heavy baking trays

non-stick Swiss roll tins

loaf tins, 500g and 1kg

cake tins in different sizes, both round and square

springform cake tins in different sizes

tart tins with detachable bases (large and individual)

pastry cutters

piping bag and tubes

steel ruler

silicone mat or non-stick baking parchment

scalpel or razor blade

pastry brush

water spray bottle or plant mister

skewer for testing cakes

wire cooling rack


**OPTIONAL, BUT HELPFUL:**

calculator

digital timer

flour bench brush

flour dredger

linen-lined baskets for proving

baking stone

deep-frying/sugar thermometer – digital is best

marble rolling sheet

large and small brioche moulds

crumpet rings

# HANDLING BREAD DOUGHS

 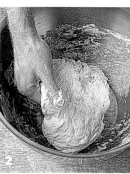

The way you handle any bread dough will determine how easily you control its shaping and development. It will also affect the rise and ultimately the baked texture. You should never be aggressive, which is why the standard British description 'knock back' is not used, since it implies a rather belligerent treatment. We encourage a more gentle approach, which pays dividends in improved elasticity by encouraging the formation of better distributed gluten strands and a better crumb in the loaf.

## Making a soft dough

Many Baker & Spice breads are the product of very wet doughs, difficult to work with and untypical in British baking. They are too sticky to knead successfully by hand and can put an intolerable strain on the motors of table-top electric mixers. We have found, however, that by repeated but minimal kneading during an extended fermentation process you can aerate and develop the dough with little effort and to remarkable effect.

Essentially, we use repeated gentle deflations of the dough during the initial rise, something described in French as *donner le tour* (to give a turn). To make life easier, we use some flour or olive oil so that you don't stick yourself to the dough. Each of the 'turns' lightly stretches the dough, as the yeast continues to work on the strands of gluten. By the last 'turn' we are left with a soft satin-like dough, free of any flour lumps and elastic to the touch.

### MIXING THE DOUGH

Place the dry ingredients in a large bowl and add the yeast liquid first, then whatever other ingredients the recipe calls for. Stir with your hands until the mixture forms a rough ball in the centre of the bowl (1, 2, 3). At first you will think the mixture is too wet and sticky, but don't worry – it is supposed to be. It's the high water content that helps give the bread its holes.

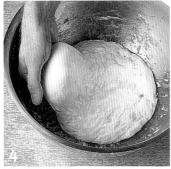

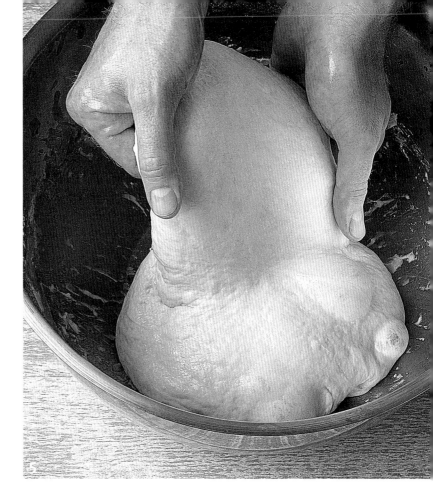

### THEN, IF THE RECIPE CALLS FOR OIL

Tip a little oil on top of the dough and rub a little on your hands before starting to tuck the dough underneath itself (1). Rotate the bowl, not the dough, and each time you do, continue tucking the dough under with your fingertips until the mass feels smoother on top (2). Cover the bowl with cling film and leave in a warm place for 45 minutes, or according to the recipe instructions. Repeat to make a satiny dough (3, 4, 5).

### OR, IF THE RECIPE USES NO OIL

Cover the work surface lightly with flour. Tip the dough on to the flour and dust the top and your hands with more flour. Now begin to tap the dough out firmly with the palm and heel of your hand until it forms a rectangle about 5cm thick. The precise size will obviously depend on the quantities in the recipe you are working from.

With the heel of your hand, pin out the dough into a rough rectangle. Fold it in half (1), then in three the other direction,

until the dough is folded like a blanket (2, 3). Dust the bowl with flour and return the dough to it. Cover and leave in a warm place for 45 minutes, or according to the recipe instructions.

Whether using the oil or flour method, repeat the action as recommended in the recipe for the duration of the fermentation. By the end you will have a lively, soft and lump-free dough.

# Kneading
# a firm dough

Kneading is not an art, but a skill that can be learned. When you watch a professional baker you will be astonished by the speed at which he works and impressed by the economy of his movements. A baker has to work fast because even in artisanal bakeries the output is staggering. Speed is not an affectation or showing off but a necessity, for without speed and focused energy the loaves would not be in the shop on time or in sufficient numbers for the customers to buy. Working in a domestic context the emphasis is not on speed – you are only going to be making a few loaves at a time – but on the kneading, and you will soon get the feeling for that. When you discover how delicious your own bread is and how little effort it takes to produce, this ceases to be a one-off exercise and you become a regular baker. Repetition and practice make for consistency in what you produce and the effort and time involved decrease. The only magic needed to create the same

 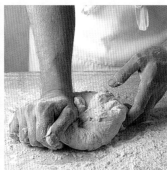  

silky-smooth dough as a professional baker is a strong but light touch and an awareness of critical stage changes in the dough as you work it.

During the kneading, you change the structure of the dough with your hands, helping to create a uniform mixture, developing and distributing the gluten strands while stimulating the yeasts. Understanding the consequences of what you are doing and why you are doing it will help you develop the perfect method to get great results every time.

### SOME BASIC RULES:

• Work quickly and on a wooden work surface if possible.
• Keep your work surface clean and dry, covered only by the lightest dusting of flour.
• Keep your hands clean and free from sticky lumps of dough.
• Dust flour on the work surface and your hands, and only on the dough if necessary.

• Be light but firm, not heavy handed. Dough is tough and resilient and you must dominate it, not the other way round.

### THE METHOD

Lightly dust the work surface with flour, and dust your hands. Tip the rough mass of dough on to the surface, then start to fold it into the centre (1). As you fold each corner in, press it down with the heel of your hand. Rotate the dough a quarter turn, then repeat the process, until all of the rough edges have been folded in (2).

Fold the dough over in half towards you, stopping it flipping back with your thumb (3). With the heel of your hand, press smoothly and gently into the mass, lifting your thumb away and turning the dough by a quarter in the same fluid movement. Do this again, concentrating on the process, the fluidity, the rhythm. Forget about the world for 10 minutes. Just concentrate on folding, pressing down and across with the heel of

your hand, turning the dough by a quarter, then repeating the action over and over. The texture will change and the dough become sticky. Then you'll need to scatter some more flour on to the surface and to dust your hands. How often you do this is not something you can write down. It comes from the feel of the dough in your fingertips.

While kneading, break off from time to time to keep the work surface clean, using a scraper to remove any lumps of dough. Add a little flour as you need to – only to the surface under the dough and to your hands. Experience will tell you how often you need to do this. Eventually the dough will become beautifully smooth and elastic (4).

# Shaping loaves

It sounds paradoxical, but there is more to shaping doughs than giving the raw dough an approximate shape which suggests that of the finished loaf. Different techniques are used to achieve different shapes, with the preliminary kneading and folding contributing to the final baked form.

### A ROUND LOAF

Tip the dough on to a lightly floured work surface. Lightly flatten with your fingertips, then fold an edge of the dough into the centre and press it down firmly. Rotate the dough 20° anticlockwise, and repeat the folding and pressing action with another edge of the dough. Continue rotating and folding until all of the edges have been folded into the centre.

Next, flip the ball of dough over so that the smooth underside is facing up. Gripping your hands around the dough, drag and turn the ball firmly across the work surface. Then pick the dough up, return it to its starting place and repeat the action a few more times. This compacts the dough and helps the strands of gluten align – which in turn helps the bread to rise dramatically in the oven during baking.

## A BAGUETTE

Place the dough on a lightly floured work surface. (Too much flour on the work surface will hinder rather than help you.) Flour your hands. Tap the dough out with your hands to flatten it slightly. Fold the top edge of the dough to the centre and fold the bottom edge up to meet it. Press down with your fingertips (1). Starting at one end, and in a continuous movement, roll the dough over towards you while closing the seam with the fingertips of your other hand as you work your way along its length (2). Repeat this action two or three times until you have a seamless, sausage-shaped coherent mass.

Finish by rolling with the palms of your hands, moving them from the centre of the loaf outwards (3) to encourage an even narrowing and lengthening of the shape (4).

## A BÂTON

Tip the dough on to a floured work surface and lightly knead into a ball. Tap out with your hands to form a rectangle. Fold the upper edge of the dough towards the centre. Press it down with your fingertips. Then fold the right and left ends of the dough in by 2cm, slightly on an angle so that the dough is vaguely triangular (1). Press these ends firmly to seal. Now fold the upper edge of the dough over to meet the lower edge and seal it down firmly with your fingers (2). Finally flip the dough around, so that the ends are reversed, and once more fold the upper edge over to meet the lower edge, sealing it down with the heel of your hand (3). Flip the shaped dough over so the seam is on top (4).

## Shaping rolls

Rolls can be shaped from virtually any
dough, though ours are typically based
on pain blanc (page 52), delivering a nice,
crisp crust with a light but chewy interior –
perfect for splitting and filling or as
breakfast or dinner rolls with butter.

## A ROUND ROLL

Weigh off a piece of dough 30–50g. Lightly flour the work surface and rub a little flour between the palms of your hands. If you are right handed, hold the dough in your left hand, cupping your right hand around the dough and working the fingers underneath (1). Now circle your right hand round and round, keeping your fingers tucked underneath. The trick is to keep the cupped palm that the dough sits in relatively free of flour, and the curved fingers and palm that press and rotate the dough well floured.

Gradually you will find that the ball of dough will tighten, and form a smooth skin on the upper surface (2). If you don't do this the roll will not hold its shape during baking. With practice, shaping a round roll should take just 5–10 seconds.

Lightly flour the cloth you will rest the dough on. Place the shaped roll with the smooth surface downward on to the floured cloth. Shape the remaining pieces and place them face down on the cloth, leaving 3cm or so between each to allow for the dough to rise and spread.

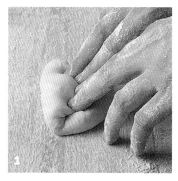
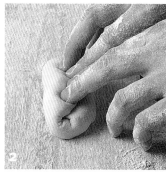

## A LONG ROLL

Weigh off a piece of dough 50–70g. Flour your hands and, on a floured surface, pat the piece of dough out into a rough rectangle. Fold the two upper corners of the dough in towards the centre, forming a triangular top with a flat base. Press these corners down firmly into the dough. Next fold the upper half down into the centre of the dough (1). With the tips of your fingers press the edge firmly down into the centre.

Flip the dough around, so that the edge that was previously at the bottom is now at the top. Again fold the top two corners in towards the centre and seal them down with your fingertips (2). Now fold the upper edge in towards the centre and seal it firmly down with your fingers. Fold the dough in half, and seal the edges together with the palm of your hand, starting at one end and working your way carefully along to the other.

Turn the shaped dough over so that the seam you have just sealed is underneath. Cup your hands over the ends of the sausage shape, clawing your fingers around the dough. Press down lightly upon the dough and rock the dough gently back and forth, increasing the pressure on the edges of your palms so that the ends of the roll are narrowed. Twist them into points.

Lightly flour a cloth and put the shaped piece of dough on it with the smooth surface downwards. Shape the remaining pieces and place them face down on the cloth, leaving 3cm or so between each to allow for the dough to rise and spread.

# Baking with wild yeasts

There are millions of microscopic yeast spores in the air. When the type called brewers' sugar fungus settles in a mixture of flour and water, slow fermentation results, during which carbon dioxide is given off and a distinct acid-sour flavour is imparted to the resulting bread. The first leavened breads were hit-or-miss affairs raised accidentally by the random colonisation and action of such airborne yeasts. It was the Egyptians who discovered 6000 years ago that the froth produced on the top of beer during fermentation when mixed into dough caused it to rise, a breakthrough that meant bakers could control the process and achieve consistent results.

Since the mid-1800s most breads have been baked using commercially produced cultured brewers' yeast which generates gas more aggressively than wild yeasts. It raises dough quickly and consequently produces sweeter, less tangy and lighter bread. Sourdough loaves, however, are still proved slowly using a starter dough colonised by wild yeasts.

# Sourdough breads

Sourdough breads are raised using the microscopic natural yeasts that are in the air all around us, and the breads get their name from the characteristic flavour they acquire during the lengthy fermentation and proving of the wheat flour dough. These are robust, rustic breads that keep well, and are often baked as very large loaves – the French oval-shaped *miche* typically weighs 2 kilos. Some cultures have always appreciated the unique taste, strong crust and chewy texture of sourdoughs. The French *pain au levain*, the Italian *pagnotta* and German rye breads are all examples of wild yeast baking at its best.

Bread has been raised using wild yeasts for at least 6000 years. How and why they made dough rise was not understood until 1857 when Louis Pasteur discovered that they generated carbon dioxide as a product of fermentation. When the type of wild yeast called brewers' sugar fungus, or brewers' yeast, settles in an appropriate environment, fermentation results, giving off carbon dioxide and delivering a distinct acid-sour flavour to the dough.

Brewers' yeast is the perfect leavening agent for strong, high-gluten bread flours because it generates gas slowly, over hours or even days. The gas is trapped as bubbles by the unique elastic and plastic qualities of the gluten, a combination of two proteins found in wheat grain. When moistened, they bind together to create thin, elastic strands. These form membranes that trap the gas, causing the dough to rise and producing leavened – as opposed to unleavened – bread. Putting raised dough in a hot oven makes the gas bubbles expand still further, and the dough cooks around them, leaving holes where the gas was and delivering light-textured loaves.

The first leavened breads were almost certainly raised accidentally by the random colonisation and action of airborne yeasts, until the Egyptians discovered that the froth produced on the top of beer during fermentation when mixed into dough caused it to rise. Other societies made the same discovery entirely independently, though much later. The Celts, for example, were found by the Romans to use beer froth, or barm, in breadmaking. In England in the twelfth century, dough was kneaded in a 'souring trough', which was never washed, so that the fermented dough left on its surface activated the next batch of dough. Beer froth continued to be widely used by bakers until the first half of the last century. Since then, most breads have been leavened using 'active', commercially produced yeast either in cultured or reconstituted dried forms. These raise dough quickly and consequently produce sweeter, less tangy and less chewy loaves.

Sourdough loaves, however, are still raised using a starter batter or dough colonised by airborne yeasts. The starter batters are called 'poolish' by bakers in the USA and Britain. This comes from the Polish

of Poland, a country renowned more for its rye baking than its sourdoughs, but which exported knowledge and technique with its bakers as they moved first through Europe and then across the Atlantic. It is the lengthy fermentation of the batter that develops the acids which give the bread its distinctive sour flavour. Levain is the term used for a naturally fermented old dough starter, the name levain being taken from the French *lever*, meaning to lift. The secret in baking these delicious and remarkable breads is in providing the right environment for the airborne yeasts to take.

The amount of sourdough poolish or levain a particular recipe needs has been adjusted to give optimum results. Many professional bakers use a strict 2 per cent of yeast to flour weight. At Baker & Spice we don't, because we feel such inflexibility only limits and restricts what can be produced. It is, however, always the start point when developing a recipe.

In the poolish recipes, precise ambient temperatures are given at different stages in the fermentation and proving process. This is not a science, however, and these are not absolutes, but the closer you can come to the recommended temperatures, the better the results will be. At all times keep the poolish out of draughts and try to avoid temperature fluctuation.

A poolish should not be cold when incorporated into a dough, so remove it from the fridge at least 2 hours before using. A levain, on the other hand, can be used straight from the fridge.

# WILD YEAST STARTERS

Making wild yeast starters is neither difficult nor time-consuming, and has a satisfying quality about it. You are simply creating an environment that airborne yeasts like. The magic is in the consequences of the fermentation this produces. Some starters can be kept going almost indefinitely – it is said that sourdough starters have been handed down from one generation to the next.

**Adding grapes or raisins to the batter will speed up the action of the airborne wild yeasts**

## San Francisco sourdough starter

**Our San Francisco sourdough starter, which is a poolish, borrows the current American artisanal bakery practice of using yoghurt, but this recipe was very much developed at Baker & Spice.**

**The poolish will raise dough as soon as the fermentation has begun; however, in the bakery we find that it takes a couple of weeks for a real flavour to develop. Sometimes bakers will give you pieces of wild yeast starter which have a developed flavour, and these can be beaten into the batter just before you add the fruit.**

**Vigorous and prolonged beating is important when making the starter because it incorporates the maximum amount of air. This will help to ensure that fermentation occurs quickly and aggressively. Later on, this vigorous activity is deliberately slowed as emphasis shifts away from the generation of carbon dioxide needed to raise the loaf and towards the development of flavour and texture in the finished bread.**

1 TABLESPOON STONEGROUND RYE OR
    WHOLEMEAL FLOUR
300G STRONG WHITE FLOUR
300G PLAIN LOW-FAT BIO YOGHURT
200ML APPLE JUICE
100G GRAPES OR RINSED AND DRAINED
    RAISINS

Put the flours, yoghurt and apple juice in the bowl of a heavy-duty electric mixer fitted with the whisk. On the slowest speed, beat for 10 minutes, when a slightly lumpy batter will have formed. Increase the speed and beat for a further 5 minutes, or until the mixture is thick, elastic and bubbly. Add the grapes or raisins, which will encourage the airborne yeasts to start working more quickly.

Pour and scrape the batter into a very clean 3 litre mixing bowl. Dust the top with a handful of white flour and cover the top of the bowl with cling film. Place the bowl in a very warm place (28°C) and leave it for

about 24 hours. This high temperature environment is necessary to kick-start the fermentation of the batter.

The next day the batter should have risen noticeably and may even have doubled in bulk. Beat for a minute with a hand whisk, then whisk in a refreshment mixture of:

150G PLAIN LOW-FAT BIO YOGHURT
150ML FULL-FAT MILK

Once completely incorporated, pour the mixture through a colander into a clean bowl and discard the fruit. Now add:

300G STRONG WHITE FLOUR

Stir the mixture together with a wooden spoon for a minute or two, breaking up any lumps of flour. Scrape down the sides of the bowl, then dust the top again with a handful of flour before covering the container with cling film. Leave it in a warm place (about 21°C) for 24 hours. You now have an active starter which can be stored in a plastic container covered with a lid in the refrigerator.

The starter can be used immediately, although it is better to wait, as it takes a couple of weeks for any special flavour characteristics to develop. Each day you need to refresh your starter – after removing 500–600g to bake with or to make American pancakes (or just discard this) – by adding the same mixture of yoghurt, milk and flour as before.

If you forget to refresh the starter, you will find that it separates and stops fermenting. It can be reactivated by beating in some more flour and yoghurt and a little apple juice. Alternatively, you can freeze the starter and then reactivate it once thawed and returned to room temperature.

# Biga acida

**The Italian version of poolish, this starter is based on 'OO' flour which you can buy from any Italian delicatessen as well as from some supermarkets.**

JUICE OF 2 ORANGES
2 TEASPOONS WHOLEMEAL FLOUR
60G 'OO' FLOUR
1 TABLESPOON RUNNY HONEY
100G STRONG WHITE FLOUR
100ML BOTTLED SPRING WATER

Put all the ingredients in the bowl of a heavy-duty electric mixer fitted with the whisk. Whisk at the slowest speed for 1 minute to mix, then increase to medium fast and whisk for 8–10 minutes.

Transfer to a large plastic container, cover and leave in a very warm place (28°C) for 24 hours. After this time the surface should be pocked with tiny holes as the yeasts start to activate. Leave for a further 24–48 hours to continue its development.

Pour the mixture into the bowl of the mixer fitted with the paddle and add the refreshment ingredients:

100ML BOTTLED SPRING WATER
150G 'OO' FLOUR

Mix at a slow speed for 3–4 minutes, then return to the plastic container, putting the lid back on. Leave at room temperature for 4–6 hours, then refrigerate overnight.

The poolish is now ready to use.

# Rye starter

Germany, like Poland, has a strong tradition of dark rye breads. The greater the percentage of rye in a dough, the darker, heavier and stronger the flavour. This starter, which is a poolish, needs quite a lot of help to get it going, and it is essential to use organic ingredients – chemicals will prevent the yeast colonisation.

After a time in the refrigerator the poolish may stop working. If it becomes sluggish and fails to double in size over 24 hours in the fridge, leave it in a warm place for 6–8 hours until it reactivates. It will gain strength from being refreshed every day.

Low-fat yoghurt is specified because less fat delivers greater activity in the dough.

125G STRONG WHITE FLOUR
125G STONEGROUND RYE FLOUR + EXTRA
    FOR SPRINKLING
150ML APPLE JUICE
150G PLAIN LOW-FAT BIO YOGHURT
50G CURRANTS, WELL RINSED AND DRAINED

In the bowl of a heavy-duty electric mixer fitted with the paddle, combine the flours, apple juice and yoghurt. Whisk at a medium speed for 10–12 minutes. Stir in the currants and transfer the mixture to a plastic container. Sprinkle the surface with a handful of rye flour to make a layer about 5mm deep. Put a lid on the container so the contents are covered but not sealed airtight, then leave in a very warm place (28°C) for 24 hours.

The next day, beat the mixture in the container for 3–4 minutes, by hand or using a spatula or fork. Sprinkle a little more rye flour on top, replace the lid and leave for another 24 hours.

Sprinkle 1–2 tablespoons rye flour on top, putting the lid back on as before. Once again, leave for 24 hours.

By the third day the mixture should be bubbly and have almost doubled in volume. Remove half of the mixture – this can be used in something like an American pancake batter or be just thrown away. Put the remaining mixture through a colander into a bowl, discarding the currants. It is now ready for the refreshment:

150ML APPLE JUICE
150G PLAIN LOW-FAT BIO YOGHURT
125G STRONG WHITE FLOUR
125G STONEGROUND RYE FLOUR

Whisk together the apple juice and yoghurt, and add to the bowl together with the flours. Stir together, then return the mixture to the plastic container. Cover with the lid and put into the refrigerator.

Each day for the next 5 days, remove half of the poolish and discard it, whisk in the same refreshment of apple juice, yoghurt and flour, then return to the fridge to ferment. By the sixth day, the poolish is ready for inclusion in dough to be baked.

# Jason's basic French levain

This is an excellent workhorse starter, reliable and easy to maintain. Levain fermentation is much slower than that which occurs with active yeast, though using organic ingredients helps the yeasts to take and gets them working more quickly. Yeasts respond well to a splash of freshly squeezed orange juice because of the vitamin C it contains. While this accelerating effect is initially desirable, the amount used in successive refreshments should be progressively reduced, as we do not want it to be too active in later stages.

You can either make this by hand or in a heavy-duty electric mixer. Using a mixer will incorporate the maximum amount of air, and with it airborne yeasts.

100G STRONG WHITE FLOUR
40G WHOLEMEAL FLOUR
3 TABLESPOONS BOTTLED SPRING WATER
1 TABLESPOON RUNNY HONEY
40ML FRESHLY SQUEEZED ORANGE JUICE

If making by hand, mound the flours on a work surface. Make a depression in the mound and carefully pour in the water, honey and orange juice. Gently combine the ingredients with your fingers. As you work, the flour and water will turn into a paste, then into a ball of dough. Now knead the dough, not too aggressively, for 7–8 minutes. When you have finished kneading, the dough will be resilient and will spring back when touched. If using a heavy-duty electric mixer, put all the ingredients in the bowl and knead with the dough hook for 8 minutes at medium speed.

This dough is now a fledgling levain. Put it in a small, clean, dry bowl, cover with cling film and leave in a warm place for 2–3 days.

When the levain is ready, there will be evident aeration and a distinctly sweet smell of fermentation, and it will have increased in size by about half (1). It is now ready for the first refreshment, which will give the yeast spores fresh material to work with.

4 TEASPOONS FRESHLY SQUEEZED ORANGE JUICE
4 TEASPOONS BOTTLED SPRING WATER
50G STRONG WHITE FLOUR
20G WHOLEMEAL FLOUR

Dilute the orange juice with the spring water, then mix with the flours on the work surface to make a loose dough. Knead this together with the active levain until the two are thoroughly integrated. Put this in a clean dry container, cover with cling film and leave in a warm place for 15–20 hours. Your levain should now have risen appreciably and be full of bubbles when you cut into it (2).

Repeat the refreshment procedure, using the same amounts, then cover the bowl with fresh cling film and leave at the same temperature to ferment for 8–12 hours. By this time the levain will have doubled in size and have a slightly sour smell and flavour. It is now ready to use for baking. If not using immediately, store in the refrigerator.

# WILD YEAST BREADS

Wild yeast breads have stronger flavours than those raised using commercial yeast. With their more robust crust and chewy, well-aerated crumb, these are loaves with real character and individuality.

# Pagnotta

A classic well-flavoured loaf, this is baked with minor regional variations throughout Italy – the Italian version of a French pain de campagne. An experienced baker used to working with wetter doughs could increase the amount of water to 150ml. The wetter the dough, the greater the aeration.

**MAKES 2 LOAVES**

500G BIGA ACIDA (PAGE 35), AT WARM ROOM TEMPERATURE
250G STRONG WHITE FLOUR + EXTRA FOR DUSTING
250G '00' FLOUR
125ML WARM BOTTLED SPRING WATER (ABOUT 20ºC)
1 TABLESPOON RUNNY HONEY
1 TABLESPOON MALDON SALT, GROUND FINE
OLIVE OIL FOR THE BOWL
POLENTA FOR THE PEEL

In the bowl of a heavy-duty electric mixer fitted with the paddle, combine the biga and flours. Whisking at slow speed, slowly add the water and beat together. Change to the dough hook. Increase the speed of the mixer to medium and beat for 8 minutes, when the biga will have broken down and the dough will be smooth and elastic. Add the honey and salt, and beat for another minute.

Rub the inside of a large mixing bowl with olive oil. Empty the dough into the bowl and turn it over several times to film the surface with oil. Cover the bowl with cling film and place in a warm part of the kitchen to prove. Leave undisturbed for 1 hour.

Transfer the dough to a lightly floured work surface. It may not have risen much by now, but the fermentation will accelerate over the next 3 hours. Dust the top of the dough and your hands with flour, then tap the dough out firmly with the palm and heel of your hand until it forms a rough rectangle. Fold in half, then in three in the other direction, until the dough is folded like a blanket. Return to the bowl, cover with cling film and leave in a warm place to prove for another hour.

Repeat the folding and deflating process each hour for the next 3 hours, re-covering the top each time with cling film.

Tip the dough out on to a floured work surface and lightly knead into a ball. Cut the dough in half. Shape each piece into a bâton (page 27). Flour two proving baskets and lay the loaves in them. Cover the baskets with a damp cloth and leave to rise in a warm place for 3–4 hours.

Preheat the oven to 250ºC, with a baking stone or heavy baking tray on the central rack.

Test to see if the dough is ready for baking by pressing a finger lightly against the surface. The dough should slowly spring back to its original shape. Dust a rimless metal sheet with polenta: this will act as the peel.

Briefly spray the baking stone or tray and the sides and bottom of the oven with water, then quickly close the oven door. Upturn one basket so the loaf falls centrally on to the peel. Lift up the loaf and stretch it about 5cm lengthways. Set it back down on the peel. Hold the loaf on its peel next to the oven, open the door and swiftly slide the loaf on to one side of the hot stone, closing the door immediately. After 2 minutes, open the oven door and spray the bread and the sides of the oven with water, again quickly shutting the door to keep heat loss to a minimum. Repeat with the other loaf. Leave to bake for 10 minutes. Turn down the oven temperature to 180ºC and bake for a further 25 minutes or until the loaves feel firm when pressed and sound hollow when tapped on the base.

Remove the bread from the oven and leave to cool to room temperature on a wire rack before slicing.

# San Francisco sourdough

San Francisco has been celebrated for its sourdough breads ever since the Gold Rush, when prospectors took pieces of starter dough from the city with them to the mountains of Northern California to bake with. This explains the name – which universally describes a loaf made primarily from white flour and raised with wild yeasts – but embraces a number of different techniques.

### MAKES 2 LARGE LOAVES

#### SPONGE

400G STRONG WHITE FLOUR
500ML WARM BOTTLED SPRING
WATER (ABOUT 20°C)
300G SAN FRANCISCO
SOURDOUGH STARTER
(PAGE 34), AT WARM ROOM
TEMPERATURE

#### DOUGH

400G STRONG WHITE FLOUR +
EXTRA FOR DUSTING
1 TABLESPOON MALDON SALT,
GROUND FINE
SEMOLINA FOR THE PEEL

Put the sponge ingredients in a bowl and mix together with a hand whisk. Cover with a damp cloth and leave in a warm place for 4–5 hours, when the sponge should be bubbling and obviously working.

Pour the sponge into the bowl of a heavy-duty electric mixer and add half the quantity of flour. Using the paddle attachment, mix together on a low speed for 2 minutes or until the mixture begins to cohere. Increase the speed to medium and beat for 8 minutes. Add the rest of the flour and the salt. Change to the dough hook and beat the dough for 8 minutes on low speed. Increase the speed to medium and beat for a further 2 minutes. You should have an elastic dough that will form a membrane when stretched between the fingers.

Tip the dough out of the bowl on to a 45 x 30cm tray. Lightly dust the top of the dough with flour, cover with a damp cloth and leave in a warm place for 1 hour. During this first fermentation, sugars are broken down and converted to carbon dioxide and alcohol. The gas provides the lift, but it is the alcohol that bonds with the gluten as organic acids, causing it to contract. This makes the dough more plastic and elastic, both resilient and stretchy.

Dust the work surface lightly with flour, and tip the dough off the tray on to it. Rub a little flour on to your hands, then pat the dough out to flatten it into a rectangle and gently deflate it. Fold in half, then in three in the opposite direction. Flip this parcel over, put it back on the floured tray and cover with a damp cloth. Leave to prove in a warm place for another hour.

Repeat the folding and deflating process every hour for 2 more hours, then tip the dough out on to the floured surface. Divide the dough into two pieces and shape each into a bâton (page 27). Line two proving baskets with a tea towel and dust generously with flour. Place the loaves in the baskets with the smooth upper surface down. Dust the loaves with more flour, then cover with another tea towel. Leave to rise in a warm place for 3–4 hours, when they will have almost doubled in bulk.

Preheat the oven to 250°C with a baking stone or heavy baking tray on the middle shelf. The plan is to bake both loaves at the same time, and to do this you need to slide the first loaf to sit on the back half of the baking stone. You can't do everything at once, so shut the oven door in between each action to keep heat loss to a minimum.

Dust two rimless metal sheets with semolina: these will act as peels. Tip one loaf from its proving basket on to a peel. Repeat with the second loaf on to the other peel. Open the oven door and slide the first loaf on to the back of the baking stone. Close the oven door while you get the second loaf, sliding this on to the front of the stone. Spray everything liberally with water, then quickly shut the oven door and bake for 10 minutes. Lower the

oven temperature to 180°C and bake for a further 40 minutes. Don't worry if the crust becomes very dark – the colour of the loaves will lighten a little after they are removed from the oven. The long bake helps the bread to keep better, preserving the texture of the crust. When done, the loaves will sound hollow when tapped on the base.

Transfer to a wire rack and leave to cool to room temperature before slicing.

# Pain au levain

**A classic, thick-crusted pain au levain is a long-lasting rustic bread. It has a terrific depth of flavour and a moist yet firm and springy crumb, with a texture more compact than some country-style breads.**

### MAKES 2 LOAVES

100G STRONG WHOLEMEAL FLOUR
400G STRONG WHITE FLOUR +
EXTRA FOR DUSTING
25G WHEAT GERM
250ML WARM BOTTLED SPRING
WATER (ABOUT 20°C)
50ML FRESHLY SQUEEZED ORANGE
JUICE
500G JASON'S BASIC FRENCH
LEVAIN (PAGE 37)
1 TABLESPOON MALDON SALT,
GROUND FINE
SUNFLOWER OIL FOR THE BOWL
SEMOLINA FOR THE PEEL

In the bowl of a heavy-duty electric mixer fitted with the paddle, combine the wholemeal and white flours, wheat germ, water and orange juice. Beat at a low speed for 6 minutes. Now add the levain and continue beating for 4 minutes. Add the salt, increase the speed to medium and beat for another 4–5 minutes. The dough should be very elastic and quite firm to the touch.

Lightly brush a 3 litre mixing bowl with sunflower oil and transfer the dough to it, covering the top with cling film. Leave in a warm place to prove for 1 hour.

Place the dough on a lightly floured surface and knead for 8–10 minutes until the mass feels soft and elastic. Clean the bowl and lightly brush with sunflower oil. Return the dough to the bowl, cover tightly with cling film and put in a warm place to prove for 2 hours.

Turn out the dough on to a lightly floured surface. With the heel of your hand, pin out the dough into a rectangle to gently deflate it. Fold in half, then in three in the opposite direction. Each time you fold, press down to remove air. Dust the bowl with flour and return the dough to it. Cover and leave in a warm place to prove for 1 hour.

Repeat the folding and deflating process, then leave to prove for a final hour.

Divide the dough into two pieces, each weighing just over 700g. Lay a clean tea towel on a small tray. Liberally dredge the towel with flour. Shape each piece of dough into a tight, round loaf (page 26) and place 'gathered' side up on the tea towel. Pull the towel up between the loaves to form little folds of cloth around them. These will steady and protect the loaves as they expand. Dust the exposed tops of the loaves with flour and cover with another tea towel. Set in a warm place to rise until doubled in size, which will take 5–6 hours.

Preheat the oven to 250°C, with a baking stone or heavy baking tray on the middle shelf.

When the oven is at the correct temperature, uncover the dough. Sprinkle a little semolina on a rimless metal sheet: this will act as your peel. Take one loaf and gently place it, gathered side down, on the peel. With a scalpel, cut 4 shallow slashes in a square shape around the loaf, about one-quarter of the way down from the top.

Open the oven door and quickly spray the hot baking stone and the sides and bottom of the oven with water, shutting the door immediately. Carry the loaf on its peel to the oven and slide it on to one end of the hot baking stone, immediately shutting the oven door. Repeat with the second loaf. After both loaves have been in the oven for 5 minutes, reduce the oven temperature to 200°C and bake for a further 55–60 minutes. When the loaves have finished baking they will be dark brown, will feel firm when pressed and sound hollow when tapped on the base.

Transfer to a wire rack to cool to room temperature before slicing.

**(Opposite) Pain au levain, top,
Bramley apple sourdough**

# Bramley apple sourdough

You do not need a lot of rye flour to make an impact – even the small amount used here gives the bread character without making it too heavy or dominant. The crumb is the perfect foil for the fruit, its sweetness balancing the acidity of the sourdough and making this a great bread to eat with cheese. This is a heavy dough, so you need an active poolish at least 4 weeks old. Extra lift can be given by the inclusion of some fast-action yeast.

Granny Smith apples can be used instead of Bramley's when the latter are not available.

**MAKES 2 LOAVES**

250G RYE STARTER (PAGE 36), AT WARM ROOM TEMPERATURE

1/2 SACHET FAST-ACTION YEAST (OPTIONAL)

200ML WARM BOTTLED SPRING WATER (ABOUT 20°C)

375G STRONG WHITE FLOUR + EXTRA FOR DUSTING

125G STRONG WHOLEMEAL FLOUR

50G RYE FLOUR

2 TABLESPOONS APPLE JUICE

2 TEASPOONS MALDON SALT, GROUND FINE

200G BRAMLEY'S APPLES (PEELED WEIGHT)

SUNFLOWER OIL FOR THE BOWL

SEMOLINA FOR THE PEEL

Whisk the starter and yeast into the warm water with half of the white flour. Cover and leave in a warm place for 1 hour or until the mixture bubbles.

Place the remaining white flour in a 4 litre bowl with the wholemeal and rye flours. Add the starter mixture, the apple juice and the salt. Stir with your hands until the mixture forms a rough ball of dough in the centre of the bowl.

Turn the dough out on to a lightly floured surface and knead for 8–10 minutes or until it feels soft and elastic. Clean the bowl and lightly brush with sunflower oil. Put the dough back in the bowl, tightly cover with cling film and leave in a warm place for 1 hour.

Peel, quarter and core the apples, then cut each quarter into 3 or 4 slices.

Turn out the dough on to the lightly floured surface. With the heel of your hand, pin out the dough into a rectangle to gently deflate it. Press the apple pieces into the dough, leaving about 2cm between them. Fold one long side in by a third, then take the opposite side and fold that over the first. Repeat the folding action with the ends. Dust the bowl with flour and return the dough to it. Cover the top with cling film and leave in a warm place to prove for 1 hour. Repeat the pinning and folding process and leave for another hour.

Turn the dough out on to the floured surface. Divide the dough into two pieces and shape each into a bâton (page 27). Lay a clean tea towel on a tray and liberally dredge it with flour. Place the loaves seam side up on the towel. Pull the towel up between the loaves to form little folds between them. These will support and separate the loaves as they expand. Dust the tops of the loaves with flour, cover with another tea towel and leave in a warm place to rise until doubled in size, which will take 2$^1$/$_2$–3 hours.

Put a baking stone or large baking tray on the central rack of the oven and preheat it to 250°C. When the oven has come up to temperature, sprinkle a little semolina on a rimless metal sheet: this will act as your peel. Gently tip one loaf top side down on to the peel. With a scalpel, cut 3 shallow slashes at an angle at regular intervals along the top.

Working quickly, spray water on the baking stone or tray and on the sides and bottom of the oven, then shut the door. Fetch the first loaf and slide it on to the baking stone. Repeat with the second loaf. After both loaves have been in the oven for 5 minutes, spray them with water and reduce the oven temperature to 200°C. Bake for a further 45–55 minutes. The loaves have finished baking when they have taken a strong colour, feel firm when pressed and sound hollow when tapped on the base.

Transfer to a wire rack to cool to room temperature before slicing.

## On bread dough

"Dough is not something that you just leave alone. It has to be nurtured. And yet there is alchemy in baking, acts of creation. You impose your will only up to a certain point because a dough can appear to have a life of its own – things will happen spontaneously.

"I use the analogy of gardening to baking – you know where you want to get to, but the plants do things that are beyond your control. There is a natural balance in bread you should never lose sight of." DAN LEPARD, BAKER

# Potato and rosemary bread

**This is adapted from a recipe given to Gail Stephens by Erez Komarovsky, whose bakery in Tel Aviv produces extraordinary sourdough breads. The Baker & Spice potato and rosemary bread retains the freshness and big flavours of the original, but it is identifiably ours.**

**MAKES 1 LOAF**

250G BIGA ACIDA (PAGE 35), AT WARM ROOM TEMPERATURE
100ML BOTTLED SPRING WATER
250G STRONG WHITE FLOUR + EXTRA FOR DUSTING
100G BAKED POTATO FLESH, CUT INTO PIECES
2 TABLESPOONS EXTRA VIRGIN OLIVE OIL + EXTRA FOR BRUSHING
1 TABLESPOON CHOPPED FRESH ROSEMARY
1 TABLESPOON BLACK ONION SEED (NIGELLA)
1 TABLESPOON MALDON SALT, GROUND FINE
SEMOLINA FOR DUSTING

Put all the ingredients except the salt into the bowl of a heavy-duty electric mixer fitted with the dough hook. Work on the slowest speed for 4 minutes, then increase to medium fast and work for a further 5 minutes, when the dough will be elastic and satin smooth. Add the salt and mix for a final 2 minutes.

Brush the inside of a 3 litre bowl with olive oil. Scrape the dough out of the mixer and into the bowl. Lightly oil your hands and rub the top of the dough. Pull the sides of the dough down and tuck them under the base, like tucking in the sheets on a bed. Repeat the movement five or six times, rotating the bowl as you do so. Cover the top of the bowl with cling film and leave in a warm place to prove for 1 hour.

Repeat the tucking process twice, proving for an hour each time.

Tip the dough on to the lightly floured surface and shape into a round loaf (page 26). Line a proving basket with a tea towel and dust generously with semolina. Place the loaf in the basket with the smooth upper surface facing down. Dust the loaf with more semolina, then cover with another tea towel. Set in a warm place to rise until doubled in size, which will take 4 hours.

Put a baking stone or large heavy baking tray on a central rack in the oven, and preheat the oven to 250°C.

Scatter semolina on a rimless metal sheet: this will act as a peel. Using the tea towel to help, roll the loaf on to your hand, then lay it, top side down, on the peel.

Spray the hot baking stone or tray and sides and bottom of the oven with water, then quickly shut the door. Leave for a minute for steam to be generated, then slide the dough off the peel on to the stone and shut the door immediately. After 5 minutes reduce the oven temperature to 200°C. Bake for a further 45–55 minutes. The bread is done when it has developed a good colour and the crust feels firm. It should sound hollow when tapped on the base.

Transfer to a wire rack and brush the top lightly with olive oil. This will give the crust an appealing shine and accentuate the colour. Cool to room temperature before slicing.

# Baking with commercial leavening

Commercial leavening describes the use of cultured bakers' yeast which, because it was first extracted from the froth that formed on the surface of beer during fermentation, is also called brewers' yeast. This is made up of the living cells of the yeast strain *Saccharomyces cerevisiae* and is usually sold as moist, compressed cakes which will keep for several weeks in a refrigerator. Although it is getting easier to buy fresh yeast, rapid fermentation and consistent results are best achieved in a domestic kitchen using sachets of dried yeast granules, variously described as fast-action, easyblend or fermipan. These can be mixed in with all the other dried ingredients, although we prefer to make a sponge of the yeast, a little flour and some liquid, as this speeds the initial fermentation and results in a better loaf.

# BREADS

Good bread is more than an accompaniment or adjunct to other foods, for it helps to shape our enjoyment and perception of the dish we are eating it with. Soup, charcuterie and cheese are all reduced in its absence. A sandwich, no matter how fine the filling, can only ever be as good as the slices of bread that define it.

## Organic wholemeal bread

**A dense-textured loaf, this slices well for sandwiches or toast. It can be tin-baked to give a traditional English shape or shaped as a free-form oval. All the ingredients in the Baker & Spice loaf are organic, though you can, of course, use non-organic materials.**

**MAKES 2 LARGE LOAVES**

1 SACHET FAST-ACTION YEAST
600ML WARM BOTTLED SPRING WATER (ABOUT 20°C)
550G STRONG WHITE FLOUR + EXTRA FOR DUSTING
500G STRONG WHOLEMEAL FLOUR
20G BRAN FLAKES
20G MALDON SALT, GROUND FINE
100ML FRESHLY SQUEEZED ORANGE JUICE
ROLLED OATS FOR COATING
SUNFLOWER OIL FOR THE BOWL AND TINS

Whisk the yeast into the warm water followed by 300g of the white flour. Leave in a warm place for 20–30 minutes or until the mixture froths.

Put all the dry ingredients, including the remaining white flour, in a 4 litre bowl. Add the yeast batter and the orange juice. Stir with your hands, mixing to form a rough ball of dough. Transfer it to a lightly floured work surface and knead for 8–10 minutes or until the mass feels soft and elastic. It is hard work, but good exercise.

Clean the bowl and lightly brush with oil. Put the dough in the bowl, tightly cover the top with cling film and leave in a warm place to prove for 1–1$^1/_2$ hours. The dough should have risen, although it won't quite double in bulk. If you cut into a corner of the dough, you should see bubbles forming inside.

Lightly oil two 1kg loaf tins. Wet a tea towel and lay it out on the work surface. Lay another tea towel next to this and sprinkle it with a layer of oats.

Turn the dough on to a lightly floured surface. Divide the dough into two pieces and shape each into a bâton (page 27). Gently roll each shaped loaf on the dampened towel to moisten it, then roll in the oats to coat all over. Drop a loaf into each prepared tin, then cover with a clean tea towel. Leave in a warm place to rise until doubled in size, which will take 1–1$^1/_2$ hours.

Preheat the oven to maximum – at least 250°C, the hotter the better.

Check the dough by poking it with a finger and watching how slowly the mark disappears. You are looking for it to come back slowly to its previous shape, but it must have some spring left in it, not an exhausted, last-gasp return. The loaves will continue to expand for the first 10–15 minutes in the oven, and will need reserves of undeveloped gluten to do this.

Spray the inside of the oven generously with water, then quickly shut the door. Carry the loaves to the oven and slide them in quickly, immediately shutting the door. After 5 minutes, reduce the oven temperature to 200°C and bake for a further 45–55 minutes or until the loaves are well coloured, have a firm crust and sound hollow when you tip them out of the tin and tap the base. Transfer to a wire rack to cool to room temperature before slicing.

# Pain blanc

The special texture of a baguette comes from slow-milled French flour T550, which is also referred to simply as baguette flour. Bakers in the UK can get it for you, though you may have to buy it in sacks, or you can, of course, buy it in France. A unique characteristic of the flour is its comparatively low rate of absorption of water.

Baguettes are made using a two-stage leavening: the sponge is made with half the amount of active yeast required, with the second half added later during kneading. The crisp crust can best be consistently achieved using T550 flour. However, while it is not authentic, we have found that a combination of low-gluten plain flour and strong flour will deliver a very acceptable baguette in a domestic oven. The trick when using soft flours for yeast dough is to keep the dough temperature quite cold. This is best achieved by mixing with cold water to compensate for the heat generated by the rapid action of an electric mixer.

Other factors critical to producing the brittle crust and light, open texture that characterise a good baguette are the initial dough temperature and the maximum heat your oven can achieve for the first 20 minutes of baking. Steam is also important, and this can be delivered by the liberal use of a spray bottle of water.

Achieving the right shape does not require the use of metal moulds – their use in large-scale commercial production is frowned upon by every artisanal baker. You can always tell a loaf proved in a mould by the tell-tale pattern of raised dots on its base. By simply rucking a cloth between pieces of dough you can achieve an authentic shape.

**SPONGE**

<sup>1</sup>/2 SACHET FAST-ACTION YEAST
175ML WARM BOTTLED SPRING
WATER (ABOUT 20ºC)
75G PLAIN WHITE FLOUR
100G STRONG WHITE FLOUR

**DOUGH**

175ML COLD BOTTLED SPRING
WATER (ABOUT 10ºC)
<sup>1</sup>/2 SACHET FAST-ACTION YEAST
250G STRONG WHITE FLOUR +
EXTRA FOR DUSTING
125G PLAIN WHITE FLOUR
10G MALDON SALT, GROUND FINE
SUNFLOWER OIL FOR THE BOWL
SEMOLINA FOR THE PEEL

Make the sponge: in a 2 litre bowl, whisk together the yeast and warm water until the yeast has dissolved. Stir in the flours. Cover the bowl with cling film and leave in a warm place for 2 hours or until the sponge has risen by at least one-third and is clearly active, with lots of bubbles.

Pour the sponge into the bowl of a heavy-duty electric mixer fitted with the whisk. Add the cold water and the second quantity of yeast, and whisk at slow speed for a minute or until the sponge is fully combined with the water. Change the whisk for the dough hook. Add the flours for the dough and work at a low speed until a rough ball of dough forms around the hook, about 2–3 minutes. Then add the salt, turn the machine up to medium fast and knead for 9–10 minutes or until the dough is smooth and quite elastic. Transfer the dough to a lightly oiled bowl and cover the top with cling film. Leave in a warm place for 30–40 minutes, just time for the dough to relax.

Tip the dough from the bowl on to a floured surface, ideally a large wooden chopping board. Divide the dough into four, each piece weighing roughly 170g. Shape each lightly into an oval and place smooth side down on a floured dinner plate. Cover with a damp cloth and set aside in a cool place to rest for 15 minutes.

Take a large tea towel or linen cloth and sprinkle flour on the surface. Lightly shake off any excess flour, then lay the cloth, flour side up, on a large tray. Pull up the cloth every 5cm to create folds about 5cm high.

Take one piece of dough and place it smooth side down on the lightly floured work surface. Shape it into a baguette (page 27). Carefully lift the loaf on to the floured cloth, setting it seam upwards in the depression of one of the folds. Repeat the shaping with the remaining pieces of dough. (Alternatively, shape into rolls, page 29.) When they are all on the floured cloth, cover them with a slightly damp cloth to protect them from the dry air. Leave to rise in a cool, draught-free place for about 2 hours or until doubled in bulk.

Put a large baking stone or heavy baking tray on a centrally positioned rack in the oven, and preheat the oven to maximum – at least 250ºC or, if possible, 280ºC.

Scatter some semolina on a rimless metal tray, which will act as your peel. Using the cloth to help you, roll the first loaf top side down on to the peel or tray. With a scalpel, cut 5–7 shallow slashes at an angle at regular intervals along the top.

Open the oven door and spray the baking stone or tray and interior of the oven with water, then quickly close the door. Carry the first loaf to the oven and slide it on to the far side of the baking stone, closing the door quickly again. Repeat with the other loaves, shutting the door in between each loading. When the baguettes have been in the oven for 3–4 minutes, spray them with water. After they have baked for 10 minutes, reduce the oven temperature to 200ºC. Bake for a further 15–20 minutes or until the baguettes have taken on a strong, golden colour, the crust feels firm and the loaves sound hollow when tapped on the base. (Rolls will take 30–35 minutes total baking time.)

Transfer to a wire rack to cool.

# French wheaten rye

This bread uses both a poolish and a small amount of active yeast to get maximum lift into the intrinsically heavy dough. It has a distinct rye taste, which is given further flavour and acidity by the wild yeast starter. In France this is the kind of bread that would be called pain de campagne, rustic, chewy and mellow.

**MAKES 1 LOAF**

1/2 SACHET FAST-ACTION YEAST
150ML WARM BOTTLED SPRING WATER (ABOUT 20°C)
200G STRONG WHITE FLOUR + EXTRA FOR DUSTING
50G RYE FLOUR + EXTRA FOR THE CLOTH
1 1/2 TEASPOONS MALDON SALT, GROUND FINE
280G RYE STARTER (PAGE 36), AT WARM ROOM TEMPERATURE
SUNFLOWER OIL FOR THE BOWL
SEMOLINA FOR THE PEEL

Make the sponge: in a large bowl whisk together the yeast and warm water until the yeast has dissolved. Stir in 150g of the white flour. Cover the bowl with cling film and leave in a warm place for 2 hours or until the sponge has risen by at least one-third and is clearly active, with lots of bubbles.

Put all the remaining ingredients into the bowl of a heavy-duty electric mixer fitted with the dough hook, and add the sponge. Turn on at medium fast speed. Mix for about 5 minutes, when the dough will have formed a rough ball. Turn the speed up to maximum and mix for a further 2 minutes. Transfer the resulting sticky dough to a lightly oiled bowl. Cover the top with cling film and put in a warm place to prove for 2 hours.

Take a large linen cloth or tea towel – about 50 x 40cm – and lay it on a tray. Rub some rye flour into it and reserve.

Tip the dough out on to a lightly floured work surface and tap it out with your hands to form a rough rectangle about 24 x 18cm. Shape into a bâton (page 27).

Put the dough, seam side down, on the floured cloth. Cover with another cloth and leave in a warm place to rise for 3 1/2–4 hours.

Preheat the oven to maximum – at least 250°C – with a baking stone or heavy metal baking tray on a centrally positioned rack. Sprinkle semolina on a rimless metal sheet to use as a peel.

Roll the loaf on to your hand, using the cloth to help, so the base is on your palm, then upend it on to one side of the peel. Working quickly, open the oven door and slide the loaf on to the stone, then immediately shut the door while you get the spray bottle. Spray the sides and bottom of the oven liberally with water, taking no more than 5 seconds over it to keep heat loss to a minimum. Shut the door immediately and bake for 10 minutes. Then lower the oven temperature to 180°C and continue baking for 40–45 minutes or until the bread is dark brown and sounds hollow when you tap the base. Transfer the loaf to a wire rack to cool to room temperature before slicing.

**Make 'fresh' breadcrumbs** from slices of day-old bread. Remove the crust, then leave uncovered at room temperature for about 24 hours to dry sufficiently to blitz in a food processor. The resulting crumbs will still have a high moisture content, so will go mouldy if put into a jar. To dry them for storage, spread them on a tray in a low oven for 1–2 hours, after which they will keep in an airtight container for several weeks.

Alternatively, put slices of bread, crusts on, on a baking tray and bake them at 150°C until browned, then blitz to a crumb. This produces raspings – the finest crumbs – best for coating fish cakes or any food that is to be egged and crumbed for deep-frying.

French wheaten rye, on left, and English granary and sunflower seed bread

# English granary and sunflower seed bread

**A loaf of pleasing textural contrasts and strong flavours, good to slice for sandwiches. The use of rye flour and malt makes for a darker colour and closer texture. Other seeds can be used instead of sunflower to ring the changes.**

**MAKES 1 LOAF**

$1/2$ SACHET FAST-ACTION YEAST
300ML WARM BOTTLED SPRING
WATER (ABOUT 20ºC)
100G STRONG WHITE FLOUR +
EXTRA FOR DUSTING
300G GRANARY FLOUR
50G RYE FLOUR + EXTRA FOR THE
CLOTH
150G JASON'S BASIC FRENCH
LEVAIN (PAGE 37)
$1/2$ TABLESPOON MALDON SALT,
GROUND FINE
75G TOASTED SUNFLOWER SEEDS
SUNFLOWER OIL FOR THE BOWL

Make the sponge: in a large bowl whisk together the yeast and 100ml of the warm water until the yeast has dissolved. Stir in the white flour. Cover the bowl with cling film and leave in a warm place for 2 hours or until the sponge has risen by at least one-third and is clearly active, with lots of bubbles.

Put all the remaining ingredients in the bowl of a heavy-duty electric mixer fitted with the dough hook, and add the sponge. Turn the mixer on at the lowest speed and work for 8 minutes, when a rough ball of dough will have formed. Turn the speed up to medium and knead for 4 minutes. Remove the dough from the bowl and put it in a lightly oiled bowl. Cover the bowl with cling film and leave in a warm place to prove for 1–1$1/2$ hours.

While the dough is proving, take a large tea towel or linen cloth and rub a little rye flour into the surface, then lay it, flour side up, on a large tray.

Tip the dough out on to a lightly floured work surface and deflate it gently by tapping it out with your hands to form a rectangle. Shape into a bâton (page 27).

Place the loaf, seam side up, on the floured cloth. Cover with another cloth and leave to rise at warm room temperature for 3$1/2$–4 hours.

Preheat the oven to maximum – at least 250ºC – with a baking stone or heavy metal baking tray set on the middle shelf. Dust a rimless metal sheet lightly with semolina, to use as a peel.

Turn the loaf out, seam side down, on to your hand, and transfer it seam side down on to the side of the peel. Open the oven door and quickly slide the loaf on to the baking stone. Shut the door and get your spray bottle. Open the door again and quickly spray the sides and bottom of the oven, taking no more than 5 seconds. Shut the oven door and leave the bread to bake for 10 minutes. Lower the oven temperature to 220ºC and bake the bread for a further 35–40 minutes or until it is dark brown in colour (the malt in the granary flour will accentuate this) and it sounds hollow when tapped on the base.

Transfer the loaf to a wire rack to cool to room temperature before slicing.

# Dan's garlic bread

**This is a remarkable bread, intense in flavour without being overpowering, sweet without being sugary, each bite a complete mouthful of contrasting textures and tastes. It is beautiful to look at, both as a whole loaf and as slices on a plate. Eat it on its own or to complement a simple, lightly dressed leaf salad.**

**MAKES 1 LOAF**

300ML WARM BOTTLED SPRING WATER (ABOUT 20ºC)
425G STRONG WHITE FLOUR + EXTRA FOR DUSTING
1 SACHET FAST-ACTION YEAST
75ML FRESHLY SQUEEZED ORANGE JUICE
100G 'OO' FLOUR
10G MALDON SALT, GROUND FINE
75ML EXTRA VIRGIN OLIVE OIL + EXTRA FOR BRUSHING
POLENTA FOR THE BAKING TRAY

**GARLIC FILLING**

3 HEADS OF GARLIC, SEPARATED INTO CLOVES
2 TABLESPOONS EXTRA VIRGIN OLIVE OIL
1–2 TABLESPOONS WATER
1 TABLESPOON BALSAMIC VINEGAR
3 TABLESPOONS CASTER SUGAR
1 TEASPOON MALDON SALT, GROUND FINE
1/4 TEASPOON BLACK PEPPER
1 SPRIG OF FRESH ROSEMARY, LEAVES PICKED AND CHOPPED

Warm a 4 litre mixing bowl with hot water. Pour in the bottled water, then whisk in half of the strong white flour and all the yeast. Leave in a warm place for 1 1/2–2 hours or until the mixture froths.

Add the orange juice, the remaining strong white flour, the 'OO' flour and salt, then stir with your hands until the mixture forms a rough ball in the centre of the bowl. The dough is supposed to be very wet and sticky: it is the high water content that helps to give the bread its open texture.

Pour a third of the olive oil on top of the dough. Rub a little on the palms of your hands, then start to tuck the dough underneath itself. Rotate the bowl in quarter turns, turning the dough over and tucking under each time, until you have a smooth, shiny mass. Cover the bowl with cling film and leave in a warm place for 45 minutes.

Lightly deflate the dough with your fingers, making dozens of indentations. Zig-zag another third of the olive oil on the surface before repeating the tucking action. Re-cover the bowl with cling film and leave in a warm place for 30 minutes. Repeat the deflating and tucking process, adding the remaining oil and then covering as before. Deflate and tuck five more times (without oil) at 30-minute intervals – a total of 3 hours. By the end the dough should be soft and smooth with no discernible floury lumps.

*continued overleaf*

For the filling, blanch the garlic in boiling water for 2 minutes, refresh briefly in cold water and peel. Put the olive oil in a small, heavy-based frying pan over a medium heat. When it shimmers, add the garlic and sauté for about a minute, being careful not to burn it. Add the water and balsamic vinegar and, as they bubble, stir in the sugar, salt, pepper and rosemary. Reduce the heat to its lowest setting and simmer for 5 minutes, when the garlic will be quite soft. Increase the heat and boil down the liquid until only a syrupy residue remains. Transfer the garlic to a bowl, scraping up all the syrup, and reserve.

Tip the dough out on to a floured surface and press out with the fingers and heels of your hands until you have a rectangle about 36 x 18cm and 2cm thick (1). Spread the cooked garlic and its syrup over the surface (2). Fold the long side furthest from you across by a third (3), then take the opposite side and fold that over the first, trapping layers of filling between the folds (4). Repeat the folding action with the ends (5, 6). Flip the dough over, cover with a damp cloth and leave to rest for 30 minutes.

Brush a large baking tray with olive oil and dust with polenta. Using a sharp knife, cut the dough parcel across into 5cm slices (7) and lay them, cut side up, in a single layer on the tray, stretching each slice slightly into an oval. You can keep the slices separate, to bake individual small loaves, or arrange them so they are touching, in which case you will have a 'pull-apart' loaf, as with hot cross buns, when baked. Cover with a damp cloth and leave in a warm part of the kitchen to rise for 1 hour or until almost doubled in size.

Preheat the oven to 250°C.

Brush the top of the loaf with olive oil. Spray the bottom and sides of the oven with water, shutting the door while you get the bread. Place it, on its baking tray, on the middle shelf. After 5 minutes, reduce the oven temperature to 180°C and bake for a further 35–40 minutes or until the loaf is quite brown and blistered, and feels firm when pressed.

Remove to a wire rack and leave to cool to room temperature before slicing.

**And next day, if there is any left over ...** Slightly stale garlic bread makes a fabulous Mediterranean-style bread-based salad like the traditional *panzanella* or *fatoush*: toast slices of bread on a ridged grill pan, tear into pieces and mix with ripe plum tomatoes, quartered, chunks of red onion and fresh basil leaves. Slices of garlic bread are also delicious fried in olive oil and served with a poached or fried egg and some shredded fresh chillies on top. And it is ideal for *l'aigo boullido*, the garlic and bread soup from Provence.

# Semolina-crust pain de mie

A separately yeasted semolina topping makes for a dramatic appearance on this bread. Pain de mie has a rich, soft interior, the crumb in marked contrast to the well-developed crust – a perfect sandwich loaf, and also ideal for bread and butter pudding.

**MAKES 2 LOAVES**

**DOUGH**

1 SACHET FAST-ACTION YEAST
250ML WARM FULL-FAT MILK
(ABOUT 20°C)
250G PLAIN WHITE FLOUR
325G STRONG WHITE FLOUR +
EXTRA FOR DUSTING
10G MALDON SALT, GROUND FINE
1$^1$/$_2$ TABLESPOONS CASTER
SUGAR
100ML COLD MILK (ABOUT 10°C)
40G UNSALTED BUTTER,
SOFTENED

**SEMOLINA TOPPING**

300ML WARM BOTTLED SPRING
WATER (ABOUT 20°C)
1 SACHET FAST-ACTION YEAST
300G SEMOLINA OR GROUND RICE
40ML SUNFLOWER OIL
40G CASTER SUGAR

Make the sponge: in a large bowl whisk together the yeast and warm milk until the yeast has dissolved. Stir in the plain flour. Cover the bowl with cling film and leave in a warm place for 2 hours or until the sponge has risen by at least a third and is clearly active, with lots of bubbles.

Add the strong flour, salt, sugar and cold milk to the sponge and start to mix. With your fingertips rub in the softened butter, a little at a time, and continue mixing to form a rough dough. Transfer this to a floured work surface and knead for 10 minutes or until the dough is very soft and pliable, and its surface feels silky to the touch. Cover the dough with cling film and leave on the work surface for 45 minutes to 1 hour.

Meanwhile, to make the topping, pour the warm water into a bowl and whisk in the yeast until it dissolves. Add the other ingredients and mix to a smooth batter. Cover the top with cling film and leave in a warm place to prove for 2–2$^1$/$_2$ hours.

Divide the dough into two pieces and shape each into a bâton (page 27).

Line a large baking tray with non-stick baking parchment or a silicone mat. Place the loaves side by side on the baking tray, about 10cm apart. Cover with cling film and leave in a warm place to rise for 1$^1$/$_2$–2 hours or until almost doubled in bulk.

Preheat the oven to 200°C.

Discard the cling film. With a skewer, lance each loaf at three points along a central line, to release any large trapped gas bubbles. Ladle half of the semolina topping over each loaf, smoothing and spreading the mixture with your hands so that the top surface is evenly covered.

Put the baking tray in the centre of the oven and bake for 15 minutes, then reduce the oven temperature to 175°C. Bake for a further 25–30 minutes or until the surface has cracked and blistered, and the loaves sound hollow when tapped on the base.

Remove the bread to a rack to cool to room temperature, then remove the excess topping from the bottom edge of the bread with scissors.

# Marmalade bread and butter pudding

Bread and butter pudding has been revived as a sumptuous dish, beloved by restaurateurs as the egg and cream element has increased and the bread content reduced to produce a set custard that is equally delicious hot or cold. This is the perfect way of using up day-old Semolina-crust pain de mie (page 61), or it can be made with Brioche (page 75). If preferred, any jam can be substituted for the marmalade, although its sharp astringency cuts and balances the sweetness and richness of the pudding well.

**SERVES 8**

575ML MILK
575ML SINGLE OR DOUBLE CREAM
1 VANILLA POD, SPLIT OPEN
ABOUT 115G UNSALTED BUTTER, SOFTENED
8 SLICES PAIN DE MIE OR OTHER WHITE BREAD, CRUSTS REMOVED
115G SEVILLE ORANGE MARMALADE
4 EGGS
2 EGG YOLKS
200G CASTER SUGAR
ICING SUGAR FOR DUSTING

Put the milk and cream in a saucepan. Scrape the sticky black seeds from the split vanilla pod into the pan and add the pod too. Set over low heat and bring slowly to the boil. Remove from the heat and leave to infuse for 30 minutes.

Meanwhile, butter the slices of bread and make 4 marmalade sandwiches. Cut them across to make triangles and arrange in a generously buttered ovenproof dish, slightly overlapping the triangles.

Beat the eggs and egg yolks with the caster sugar in a bowl until they form a smooth, foaming mixture. Pour the milk and cream mixture through a sieve on to the eggs and sugar, whisking to make a smooth custard. Ladle this carefully over the bread and leave to soak for 30 minutes.

Preheat the oven to 160°C. Place the dish in a bain marie and pour in hot water to come half-way up the sides of the baking dish. Bake for 45 minutes or until the pudding is firm but still with some give to the gentle pressure of a finger.

Serve warm or refrigerate overnight and serve very cold. In both cases, dust the top with icing sugar before serving. Blueberries or raspberries go well with this.

# FLAT BREADS AND SHAPED DOUGH

Many flat breads, such as carta musica or tortillas, do not contain yeast. The flat breads here, while raised with active yeast, are distinguished from the majority of leavened breads in that the height or thickness of the bread is deliberately restricted, with the loaves having a much larger surface area in proportion to their depth.

## Roquefort and walnut fougasse

**The basis for the fougasse of Provence is, in fact, a north-western Italian flat bread. Fougasse is a pretty bread distinguished by its slashed holes. Traditionally in a ladder or tree shape, the slashes may also be cut through the loaf in a rough herringbone pattern. Originally a sweet bread eaten as a dessert, fougasses are now more often plain or savoury.**

**MAKES 3 FOUGASSES**

**SPONGE**

170ML WARM BOTTLED SPRING WATER (ABOUT 20°C)
170G STRONG WHITE FLOUR
$^1/_2$ SACHET FAST-ACTION YEAST

**DOUGH**

270ML WARM BOTTLED SPRING WATER (ABOUT 20°C)
$^1/_2$ SACHET FAST-ACTION YEAST
450G STRONG WHITE FLOUR + EXTRA FOR DUSTING
120G RYE FLOUR
10G MALDON SALT, GROUND FINE
1 TABLESPOON EXTRA VIRGIN OLIVE OIL + EXTRA FOR BRUSHING

**ROQUEFORT AND WALNUT FILLING**

200G ROQUEFORT, CRUMBLED
150G WALNUTS, TOASTED IN A 180°C OVEN, THEN ROUGHLY CHOPPED

Make the sponge (the fermented starter): put the water in a large bowl and mix in the flour and yeast. Keep mixing for 3–4 minutes or until a smooth batter has formed. Cover with cling film and let the sponge sit in a warm place for $1^1/_2$–2 hours or until it looks active and full of bubbles.

To make the dough, add the water and yeast to the sponge. Then add the flours, salt and olive oil, and mix to a rough dough. Turn the dough out on to a floured work surface and knead for 5–8 minutes to form a soft, smooth dough. Transfer this to a clean, dry container, cover with a damp cloth and leave in a warm place for 30 minutes.

Return the dough to the floured work surface and pin it out into a rectangle to deflate it. Cover the surface with the Roquefort and walnuts, then gently fold the edges of the dough into the middle so that the filling is enclosed. Repeat the pinning and folding action several times. By this time the filling should be evenly distributed through the dough. (For a plain fougasse, omit the filling, but fold as described.) Transfer to a bowl, cover with cling film and leave in a warm place to prove for 45 minutes.

Divide the dough into three equal pieces and shape each into a ball. Leave to rest on the floured work surface, covered with a damp cloth, for 15 minutes. Then roll each piece of dough out into an oval about 25–30cm long and 10–12cm wide. Cut 8 or 9 deep slashes in each oval, cutting at an angle. Transfer the fougasses to baking trays lined with non-stick baking parchment or a silicone mat, cover with cling film and leave to rise at room temperature for at least 1 hour.

Preheat the oven to 220°C.

Brush the fougasses generously with extra virgin olive oil. Bake for 15–20 minutes or until well coloured, with a firm crust. The bread should sound hollow when tapped on the base. Cool on a wire rack.

**(Opposite, from top left) Roquefort and walnut fougasse, Focaccia and Roast pepper and paprika bread**

# Roast pepper and paprika bread

Paprika, originally a Hungarian spice, is the fine powder made from a dried variety of sweet red pepper which, although it looks like a large chilli, has no heat. A similar though different-tasting spice is made in Spain where it is called pimentón. Either paprika or pimentón can be used for this recipe. It is worth investing in a good example as there are many poor quality red pepper powders passed off as the real thing – if it is cheap it is almost certainly not worth buying. Paprika and pimentón should be a dark, brick-red colour and have a strong, smoky smell. If the spice is brown rather than red, it is stale and should not be used.

3 LARGE RIPE RED PEPPERS
370ML WARM BOTTLED SPRING
WATER (ABOUT 20ºC)
$^1$/2 SACHET FAST-ACTION YEAST
575G STRONG WHITE FLOUR +
EXTRA FOR DUSTING
10G MALDON SALT, GROUND FINE
50ML EXTRA VIRGIN OLIVE OIL
1 TEASPOON PAPRIKA, DISSOLVED
IN 50ML EXTRA VIRGIN
OLIVE OIL
SEMOLINA FOR THE BAKING TRAY

One at a time, thread the peppers on to a metal skewer and, holding the end in a cloth or oven glove, turn over a flame until the skin blisters all over and begins to char. (If you do not have gas, turn the peppers frequently under a preheated hot grill.) Put the peppers in a bowl and cover tightly with cling film. As soon as they are cool enough to handle, strip off the skin, working from the stalk end and using a small, sharp knife to lift and pull with. Cut the peppers in half lengthways and scrape out the seeds. Cut out the cores and white ribs. Set the peppers aside.

In the bowl of a heavy-duty electric mixer, whisk together the water, yeast and half the flour. Cover the top of the bowl with cling film and leave in a warm place for $1^1$/2–2 hours or until the mixture froths.

Place the remaining flour in a 4 litre bowl and add the yeast mixture, the salt and oil. Fit the dough hook to the mixer and knead the dough for 3 minutes on a slow speed, then increase the speed to medium fast and briskly beat the dough for 8–9 minutes or until it is very smooth and elastic and has a satin feel. Cover the bowl with cling film and leave in a warm place to prove for 45 minutes.

Tip the dough out on to a floured work surface. Lightly sprinkle a little flour over the surface of the dough, and rub a little more on your hands. Tap the dough out firmly with the palm and heel of your hand until it forms a rough rectangle. Fold in half, then in three in the other direction, until the dough is folded like a blanket. Each time you fold, press down to remove air. Dust the bowl with flour and return the dough to it. Cover and leave in a warm place to prove for 30 minutes. Repeat the folding and deflating every 30 minutes for a total of 3 hours. By now the dough should be soft, aerated and smooth.

Tip the dough out on to the floured surface. Shape it into a rough ball, leaving it seam side down. Cover with a cloth and leave to rest for 15 minutes.

Flip the ball of dough over smooth side down on the lightly floured work surface. Tap the dough out with the palms of your hands to flatten it slightly, then shape it into a bâton (page 27). Cover the dough and leave on the work surface to rest for 15 minutes.

Now roll out one long side of the loaf with a rolling pin, creating a rounded, flat end that extends away from the rest of the loaf and is large enough to fold back and wrap round the piece which will form the base. With your fingertips indent the surface of the base only. Take the pepper halves and lay them over the indentations, leaving a 2cm edge uncovered. Brush the peppers with a little of the paprika oil.

With a scalpel, slash through the rolled-out lid, creating a herringbone of cuts. Carefully lift this and wrap it over the top of the loaf, so that the peppers are slightly exposed through the lattice. Tuck around the dough so that the lattice is firmly in place. Line a heavy baking tray with non-stick baking parchment or a silicone mat and sprinkle with semolina. Transfer the loaf to the tray. Leave in a warm part of the kitchen to rise for 45 minutes to 1 hour or until almost doubled in size.

Preheat the oven to 250ºC.

Brush the top of the loaf with the remaining paprika oil. Bake for 15 minutes, then reduce the oven temperature to 180ºC and bake for a further 30–35 minutes or until the loaf is well browned and slightly blistered and feels firm when touched.

Remove from the tray and leave to cool on a wire rack.

# Focaccia

**Focaccia is described as an Italian flat bread, a rather confusing description since it is leavened using active yeast. However, it is spread out and baked on trays or in tins, which gives it a characteristic rectangular shape, the top marked with regular depressions. It turns a beautiful golden brown from the liberal dressing with olive oil it receives just before going in the oven. A common mistake is to incorporate too much olive oil into the dough itself, leading to a poor rise and an oily finish. Focaccia is always well salted on the surface and often includes rosemary.**

### MAKES 2 FOCACCIA

1 SACHET FAST-ACTION YEAST
680ML WARM BOTTLED SPRING
WATER (ABOUT 20°C) +
1–2 TABLESPOONS MORE
WATER IF REQUIRED
1KG STRONG WHITE FLOUR +
EXTRA FOR DUSTING
20G MALDON SALT, GROUND FINE
1 TEASPOON CASTER SUGAR
1 TABLESPOON OLIVE OIL + MORE
FOR BRUSHING

### TO FINISH

LEAVES FROM 2 SPRIGS OF FRESH
ROSEMARY (ABOUT 1 HEAPED
TABLESPOON), OPTIONAL
75ML EXTRA VIRGIN OLIVE OIL
COARSE MALDON SEA SALT

Make the sponge: in a large bowl whisk together the yeast and the warm water until the yeast has dissolved. Stir in 500g of the flour. Cover the bowl with cling film and leave in a warm place for 2 hours or until the sponge has risen by at least one-third and is clearly active, with lots of bubbles.

Put the remaining flour in the bowl of a heavy-duty electric mixer fitted with the dough hook and add the sponge, salt, sugar and oil. Mixing at the lowest speed, work for 7 minutes. If the dough is too stiff, add a little more water, 1 tablespoon at a time. It should be firm and slightly sticky. Increase to full speed and beat for 1 minute, when you should have an elastic dough that is resilient to the push of a finger and which springs back when you stop pushing.

Turn out on to a floured surface and shape into a ball. Oil a bowl large enough to allow the dough to treble in size. Put the dough in and brush the top with a little more olive oil. Cover the top with cling film and put to prove in a cool, draught-free place for about 2 hours. The dough will be moist, sticky and elastic when you take it from the bowl.

Transfer to a heavily floured work surface. Tap the dough out firmly with the palm and heel of your hand until it forms a rough rectangle. Fold in half, then in three in the other direction, until the dough is folded like a blanket. Divide it in half, and tap and press out each piece into a rectangle again. Transfer to 2 floured non-stick Swiss roll tins, each measuring about 30 x 20cm, and push out to fill the tins evenly. Cover each tin with a cloth and leave to rise at room temperature for 1 hour.

Preheat the oven to 250°C.

With the tips of your fingers, poke holes in the dough to dimple the surfaces comprehensively in straight lines. Sprinkle on the rosemary, if using. Zig-zag the olive oil over and scatter coarse salt on top. Bake in the centre of the oven for 10 minutes, then turn the temperature down to 200°C. Continue baking for 15–20 minutes, when the focaccia will have risen to a height of about 4–5cm. Remove and leave to cool in the tins. To serve, cut in squares.

**Rolled out to thin rounds,** focaccia dough is perfect as a pizza base. Keep toppings to a minimum – the best pizzas have the most basic and simple toppings, like a classic margherita of tomato, mozzarella and basil. For baking pizzas, a very hot oven and a baking stone are ideal, though metal pizza trays also work well. Allow about 8 minutes in the oven.

# Pretzels

Our pretzels are big, New York-style twists of pagnotta dough dusted with sesame seeds or zatar, baked golden crisp but with a nicely light-textured crumb. Zatar is a Middle Eastern spice mix given a characteristic sour edge by sumak – a red powder made from the dried berries of the shrub of that name, which is used extensively in Iraqi cooking. To make zatar, mix together equal amounts of powdered sumak and ground dried marjoram and thyme.

**MAKES 1 BIG PRETZEL**

200G PAGNOTTA DOUGH (PAGE 39) OR FOCACCIA DOUGH (PAGE 68), AFTER PROVING IS COMPLETED AND THE DOUGH IS READY TO SHAPE

STRONG WHITE FLOUR FOR DUSTING

SUNFLOWER OIL AND SEMOLINA FOR THE PEEL

**TO FINISH**
1 EGG
1 TABLESPOON WATER
1–2 TEASPOONS ZATAR OR SESAME SEEDS

On a heavily floured surface, roll the dough into a cylinder about 50cm long. Turn this to make a loop, as if making the first move when tying a tie. You will have an oval with one piece of dough crossing over itself, like a lapel ribbon. Twist the loop in the middle to give two equal loops above the crossed-over tails of the dough. Bring the tails up and over the loops, pressing down.

Flour a cloth-lined tray. Transfer the pretzel to the tray. Cover with another cloth and leave to rise in a warm place for 30 minutes.

Preheat the oven to 220°C, with a baking stone or heavy metal baking tray on the middle rack. Lightly brush a rimless metal sheet with oil and dust with semolina: this will act as a peel.

During the rise the pretzel will have contracted as well as expanded. Tug and stretch it gently to restore its shape. Transfer to the peel. Lightly beat the egg with the water and brush this over the pretzel. Scatter the zatar or sesame seeds on top. Slide the pretzel on to the baking stone and bake for 40–45 minutes.

Remove to a wire rack to cool.

# Grissini

**Grissini – crisp bread sticks – were first made in Turin and remain a speciality of that city's small street bakeries. They bear little resemblance to mass-produced grissini, which are machine-made, identical, smooth and snapping to a tongue-drying dust in the mouth. Turin's grissini are closer to loaves, and some are up to a metre long.**

MAKES ABOUT 25 GRISSINI
(ABOUT 25CM LONG)

1 RECIPE PAGNOTTA DOUGH
(PAGE 39) OR FOCACCIA
DOUGH (PAGE 68), AFTER
PROVING IS COMPLETED AND
THE DOUGH IS READY TO
SHAPE
STRONG WHITE FLOUR FOR
DUSTING
SEMOLINA FOR DUSTING

TO FINISH (OPTIONAL)
50ML EXTRA VIRGIN OLIVE OIL
CHOPPED FRESH THYME,
ROSEMARY OR OREGANO
25G COARSE MALDON SALT
COARSELY GROUND BLACK PEPPER

On a floured work surface flatten the dough out with your hands. Lightly flour the surface of the dough, then roll out with a rolling pin into a long rectangle, as thin as you can. The dough will reach a point when it resists your best efforts and shrinks back. When this happens, cover with a tea towel and leave it to rest for 15–20 minutes. Then resume rolling, resting the dough, covered, a second time. On the third rolling you should have a rectangle about 8–10mm thick.

Line two baking trays with non-stick baking parchment or a silicone mat and sprinkle with semolina. With a sharp knife, roughly cut the dough rectangle into 1cm wide lengths. Make lengthways cuts in one end of each strip of dough, if you like. Transfer them as you cut to the baking trays, leaving space between them. When you have used up all the dough, cover the trays with cling film and leave to rise at warm room temperature for 45 minutes to 1 hour.

Preheat the oven to 200°C. If you like, you can lightly brush the tops of the grissini with a little olive oil, then sprinkle them with a few chopped herbs, sea salt or black pepper – whatever takes your fancy. At Baker & Spice the grissini are kept plain, covered only with a light dusting of flour.

Place the trays in the oven and bake for 20–30 minutes or until the grissini are lightly coloured and crisp. Once removed from the oven, transfer to a wire rack to cool.

# SWEET YEASTED BAKING

The tradition of baking sweet yeasted doughs enriched with eggs and butter is almost as old as leavened bread. The products can range from relatively simple spice breads with festive calendar associations, like hot cross buns and pain d'épices, to sophisticated and luxurious brioches.

## Hot cross buns

**Sweet, moist, spicy and studded with fruit, hot cross buns are that British rarity – a seasonally baked speciality. Of course they are just as nice without their piped Easter cross at any time of the year.**

**Makes 24 buns**

1 sachet fast-action yeast
200ml warm bottled spring water (about 20°C)
870g strong white flour + extra for dusting
230ml cold bottled spring water (about 10°C)
25g skimmed milk powder
100g caster sugar
15g Maldon salt, ground fine
85g unsalted butter, softened
1 egg
40g ground mixed spice
100g raisins
70g dried apricots, chopped
80g candied citrus peel, chopped

**Piping paste**

4 tablespoons plain white flour
1 tablespoon caster sugar
1 tablespoon cold water

**Glazes**

1 egg yolk
1 tablespoon milk
100g sugar
50ml water

Make the sponge: in a large bowl whisk together the yeast and the warm water until the yeast has dissolved. Stir in 200g of the flour. Cover the bowl with cling film and leave in a warm place for 2 hours or until the sponge has risen by at least one-third and is clearly active, with lots of bubbles.

Put the remaining flour in the bowl of a heavy-duty electric mixer fitted with the dough hook and add the sponge, cold water, milk powder, sugar, salt, butter, egg and mixed spice. Switch on at the lowest speed and work for 8 minutes, when you will have a very soft dough. Add the fruit and candied peel, turn up the speed to medium and knead for 1 minute only. Remove the dough to a floured work surface and knead for 1 minute, then form a ball. Put into a bowl, cover with cling film and leave to prove in a warm place for 45 minutes to 1 hour or until doubled in bulk.

Turn out on to the lightly floured work surface and gently press out into a rectangle to deflate. Weigh the dough, then divide into 24 equal pieces, using the scales to be precise. Form each piece into a neat ball. Line baking trays with non-stick baking parchment and arrange the balls on the trays in lines, almost but not quite touching. Cover with a slightly damp cloth and leave in a warm place to rise for 45 minutes or until the buns have doubled in size and joined together as they have expanded.

Half-way through the rise, preheat the oven to 250°C. Also, make the piping paste for the crosses by mixing the flour and sugar with the water. Put into a piping bag fitted with a small, plain nozzle. Beat the egg yolk and milk together for a glaze.

Using a skewer or a blunt knife, indent a cross on the top of each bun. Brush with the egg glaze, then pipe a cross in the indentation. Put the buns in the oven, turning the temperature down to 180°C as soon as you shut the door. Bake for 30–40 minutes or until the buns are golden and darkening around the outside edges. Like bread rolls, they will sound hollow when tapped on the base.

Transfer to a wire rack. Dissolve the sugar in the water and bring to the boil. Brush this glaze over the buns. Resist the temptation to pull them apart until they have cooled to room temperature.

# Brioche

**Brioche is the most luxurious of breads, made rich and yellow with butter and eggs. This enrichment gives it a close texture, more like a cake than a bread. It is usually eaten at afternoon tea as a cake or at breakfast, but when sliced and toasted also forms the classic accompaniment to a foie gras terrine. Some brioche recipes are very rich, with equal parts flour and butter, but you will get a more consistent result using half the weight of butter to flour.**

**MAKES 2 LARGE BRIOCHES OR 16 INDIVIDUAL BRIOCHES**

1 SACHET FAST-ACTION YEAST
500G STRONG WHITE FLOUR +
EXTRA FOR DUSTING
50ML WARM BOTTLED SPRING
WATER (ABOUT 20°C)
15G MALDON SALT, GROUND FINE
75G CASTER SUGAR
5 EGGS
250G UNSALTED BUTTER,
SOFTENED
MELTED BUTTER AND FLOUR
FOR THE TINS

**GLAZE**
2 EGG YOLKS
2 TABLESPOONS MILK OR WATER

Make the sponge: dissolve the yeast and 25g of the flour in the warm water. Cover and leave in a warm place for 30–40 minutes or until bubbling and clearly active.

Place the remaining flour in the bowl of a heavy-duty electric mixer fitted with the paddle and add the sponge, salt, sugar and eggs. Mix at low speed until the dough comes together – about 7 minutes. Add the butter, increase the mixer speed to medium and continue to mix for about 15 minutes, when the butter will be fully incorporated and the dough will be shiny and elastic. Transfer the dough to a lidded plastic container or cling-wrapped bowl and refrigerate overnight.

Put the dough on a floured work surface. Divide it in half, or into 16 pieces weighing 60g each (for individual brioches). Shape each piece into a ball and leave to rest for 20 minutes.

For each large brioche: divide the ball of dough into two pieces, one about one third of the total amount. Shape the larger piece of dough into a ball, then make a hole in the centre of the top with your finger and push down until you break through the bottom. Stretch the hole with your fingers until you have a rather fat and tall ring doughnut. Now shape the smaller piece into a cylinder tapered at one end. Cut through the tapered end from its end to half-way up. You should have a shape that looks a little like a tooth, with the split tapered end forming its roots. Place this end into the hole in the doughnut, pulling the roots through and tucking them under the base. This will ensure that the head of the brioche rises straight upwards, and does not lean to one side. Tuck the top edge of the doughnut back into the hole; this will keep the two pieces together as the brioche rises.

For each individual brioche: using the edge of your outstretched hand like a knife, make an indentation in the ball of dough to measure off about a third of the diameter. Lightly grip the large end of the dough ball with your other hand, and rock the dough back and forth, separating a smaller ball joined by a thread to the larger ball. Then carefully turn the large ball upright and shove your fingers into the top to make an indentation. Place the smaller ball of dough into it, coiling the joining thread underneath into the hole.

Lightly brush two fluted brioche tins (or 16 individual tins) with melted butter and dust over that with a little flour. Place the moulded brioches firmly inside the tins. Leave to rise in a warm place for 3–4 hours or until doubled in bulk.

Preheat the oven to 200°C.

For the glaze, lightly beat the egg yolks with the milk or water. Brush the top of the brioches with the glaze. Bake for 10–15 minutes, then reduce the heat to 180°C. For large brioches, bake for a further 35–40 minutes, or 15–20 minutes for individual ones, or until risen and a good golden brown.

# Fig and brioche tart

The amount of filling here may seem inadequate, but the brioche dough swells and rises so much it would squeeze any larger amount out. The tart is best on the day of baking.

**MAKES A 22CM TART**

250G BRIOCHE DOUGH (PAGE 75), AFTER PROVING IS COMPLETED AND THE DOUGH IS READY TO SHAPE
7–8 FRESH RIPE FIGS
60G PLAIN LOW-FAT BIO YOGHURT
60G CASTER SUGAR
60ML DOUBLE CREAM
4 EGG YOLKS
GRATED ZEST OF 1/2 LEMON
SCANT 1 TABLESPOON CORNFLOUR

Preheat the oven to 180°C.

Roll the brioche dough out to a thickness of 4–5mm and use to line a lightly oiled 22cm fluted round tart tin that is 2.5cm deep, preferably one with a removable base. Take the halved figs and place them, cut side up and slightly overlapping, on the dough. Put all the remaining ingredients in a bowl and mix thoroughly. Pour this custard over and around the figs.

Place in the oven and bake for 15 minutes. Reduce the oven temperature to 150°C and bake for a further 35–40 minutes or until the brioche is risen and golden brown and the filling just set. Check after 25 minutes – if it looks as if it is browning too quickly, cover it with a small sheet of foil.

Leave to cool to room temperature and then serve.

# Prune clafoutis

Clafoutis was originally a dessert from Limousin in central France that featured the tiny black cherries the region is famous for. It can also be made with halved plums or apricots when they are at their seasonal best. Prunes – sweet dried plums – are available all year round and, enlivened with a little brandy and sugar, make a particularly good clafoutis. The best prunes to use are from Agen, though if you cannot get any, Californian ready-to-eat prunes are widely available and very good.

A clafoutis is traditionally made without pastry, but the batter can be baked in a sweet pastry case (page 131) to make a delicious and different tart that eats well with whipped cream.

**SERVES 6**

400G STONED PRUNES
50ML BRANDY
50G CASTER SUGAR

**BATTER**
125G PLAIN FLOUR
150ML FULL-FAT MILK
50ML DOUBLE CREAM
30G UNSALTED BUTTER
2 EGGS
50G CASTER SUGAR
BUTTER AND FLOUR FOR THE BAKING DISH

If using prunes that need to be rehydrated, put to soak overnight in an infusion of weak, sugared tea. Drain, then put back in the bowl, add the brandy and sugar, and toss to coat evenly. Leave to macerate for 2–3 hours at room temperature.

Preheat the oven to 180°C. Grease a 30 x 20cm baking dish with butter, then dust lightly with flour and reserve.

Sift the flour into a bowl. In a pan, heat the milk and cream together until hot but not boiling. Remove from the heat and add the butter, then leave it to melt.

With a hand-held electric mixer or whisk, beat the eggs and sugar together until pale and creamy, then add the milk mixture. Stir in gently with a spoon. Fold in the flour to make a smooth, soft batter. Do not beat hard as this would toughen the cooked mixture and affect the rise.

Drain the prunes and distribute them evenly in the prepared dish. Pour over the batter. Bake for 40–45 minutes or until the batter has risen up around the prunes and the surface has a nice golden colour.

Fig and brioche tart, top, and Prune clafoutis

# Crumpets

Crumpets have been an English tea-time favourite since the early seventeenth century. Then they were made from buckwheat flour, which makes them sound similar to blinis, the small Russian yeast pancakes served with caviar. In 1769 Elizabeth Raffald described crumpets made with wheat flour in a batter raised with a sourdough starter, cooked on a griddle before being toasted before an open fire. The crumpet's popularity reached its zenith in the 1920s and '30s, when afternoon tea would not have been complete without hot buttered crumpets and jam.

Crumpets are traditionally cooked on a flat griddle, though you can also use a heavy-based frying pan or a non-stick pan. Difficulties may come from using too much yeast, from having too solid a batter or from cooking at the wrong temperature. To make crumpets properly you will need some 8.75cm metal crumpet rings (or straight-sided metal pastry cutters) to put on to the flat metal surface on which you cook them.

**MAKES 12 CRUMPETS**

450G PLAIN FLOUR
1 TEASPOON CASTER SUGAR
1 SACHET FAST-ACTION YEAST
350ML SKIMMED MILK
350ML BOTTLED SPRING WATER
1 TEASPOON MALDON SALT,
GROUND FINE
1/2 TEASPOON BICARBONATE OF
SODA
SUNFLOWER OIL

Sift the flour into a bowl with the sugar and yeast. Warm the skimmed milk and water to about 20°C, then use a hand whisk to beat this liquid into the flour to make a smooth batter. Cover the bowl with cling film and leave to stand at room temperature for about 2 hours. The batter will more than double in size before falling slightly.

Beat in the salt and bicarbonate of soda. Leave to rest for 10 minutes while you heat a griddle or heavy frying pan over a low flame.

You must now judge whether your batter is the right consistency, which should be like that of unwhipped single cream. If too thick, the honeycomb of holes, which is the defining point of the crumpet, will not occur. If too thin, the batter will run from under the rings. If the cooking surface is too hot, the batter will burn before the crumpet is ready to be turned; if too cool, the crumpet will rise incompletely and be leaden. Test both batter and heat of pan by cooking a spoonful of batter before proceeding. If the batter is too thick, thin with a little water; if too thin, beat in a little more flour.

Moisten a piece of kitchen paper with oil and rub over the inside of the metal rings and the hot surface of the griddle, placing the rings on top. Put 3 tablespoons of batter into each ring. Cook for 6–8 minutes or until the surface is set and filled with holes. Turn the crumpets and rings over with a palette knife or spatula and cook for a further 2–3 minutes. The first side should be a chestnut brown, the second only barely coloured, and the crumpets about 3cm thick. Lift off the rings with a cloth. Eat at once, or leave to cool and then toast the pale side. Serve with butter and jam or honey.

# Doughnuts

The two keys to successful doughnuts are a properly proved sweet yeast dough and clean oil at the right temperature. This is 190°C, the temperature at which the exterior of the doughnut is sealed, preventing excessive fat absorption, and hot enough to cause the carbon dioxide gas trapped inside the dough to expand rapidly, giving the right, airy light texture. Frying a yeasted dough gives a completely different exterior finish to baking and a lovely, uniform golden brown colour. Before you begin, change the oil in the fryer and clean the interior. Any neutral-tasting oil, like sunflower, will do.

**MAKES 20 DOUGHNUTS**

1 SACHET FAST-ACTION YEAST
175ML WARM MILK (ABOUT 20°C)
170G PLAIN WHITE FLOUR
280G STRONG WHITE FLOUR +
EXTRA FOR DUSTING
1 TEASPOON MALDON SALT,
GROUND FINE
85G UNSALTED BUTTER, DICED
AND SOFTENED
2 EGGS, BEATEN
85G CASTER SUGAR + EXTRA FOR
COATING
GRATED ZEST OF 1 LEMON
1 TEASPOON GROUND CINNAMON
SUNFLOWER OIL FOR BRUSHING
OIL FOR DEEP FRYING

Make the sponge: in a large bowl whisk together the yeast and the warm milk until the yeast has dissolved. Stir in the plain flour. Cover the bowl with cling film and leave in a warm place for 2 hours or until the sponge has risen by at least one-third and is clearly active, with lots of bubbles.

Put the strong flour in the bowl of a heavy-duty electric mixer fitted with the dough hook and add the sponge and salt. Turn on at the lowest speed. Add the butter one piece at a time. When fully incorporated, add the beaten eggs, one at a time. Add the sugar, grated lemon zest and cinnamon, and knead for 8 minutes. Turn to full speed and knead for a further 2 minutes.

Turn the sticky dough out on to a heavily floured surface and finish kneading by hand, incorporating additional flour until you have a smooth, elastic ball of dough. Brush this with a little oil and place in a lightly oiled bowl. Cover with cling film. Leave to prove at room temperature for 2 hours or until at least doubled in size.

Turn the dough on to the floured surface and gently press out to a rectangle. Divide into 20 equal pieces, rolling them into balls. If you want to make ring doughnuts, make a hole in the centre of each ball by pushing your finger through, then circle your finger to enlarge the hole to about 2cm in diameter. Put the doughnuts on a floured tray and cover with a cloth. Leave to rise in a warm place for 40–50 minutes or until doubled in size.

Heat oil for deep frying to 190°C. Fry the doughnuts in small batches, being careful not to overcrowd the pan as this will cause the temperature of the oil to drop below sealing point. Fry for 1–2 minutes on the first side, then turn and give them a further minute on the other side. When done, drain on kitchen paper.

Put some caster sugar on a plate and turn the doughnuts in this to coat while still warm. Serve as soon as possible – they are best eaten minutes from the pan.

# Plum fritters

Fritters may be savoury or sweet. They are made either by mixing chopped elements into a fairly thick batter or by dipping larger pieces into a thinner, coating batter. In both cases they are deep-fried. Our fritters are filled with seasonal fruit, and the dough is quite wet so it moulds round the fruit easily. Ripe Victoria plums make great fritters, although they can be made using a variety of fruit – really anything that is not too wet. Fritters are best enjoyed still warm – and certainly never more than 2 hours from their frying.

Amounts for the dough can be doubled, but if you do this, still use the same amount of yeast.

**MAKES 8 FRITTERS**

300ML WARM BOTTLED SPRING WATER (ABOUT 20°C)
1 SACHET FAST-ACTION YEAST
125G PLAIN WHITE FLOUR + EXTRA FOR DUSTING
170G STRONG WHITE FLOUR
15G CASTER SUGAR + EXTRA FOR DREDGING
GRATED ZEST OF 1 LEMON
1 TEASPOON MALDON SALT, GROUND FINE
4 RIPE PLUMS
OIL FOR DEEP FRYING

Put the warm water in the bowl of a heavy-duty electric mixer fitted with the dough hook. Add the yeast and switch on at low speed, then add all the remaining ingredients except the plums. Work for 10 minutes to produce a shiny, thick batter. Alternatively, make the batter using a hand whisk. Cover the top of the bowl with cling film and leave to prove in a warm place for 2 hours.

Heat oil for deep frying to 190°C.

Cut the plums in half and discard the stones. Add the plums to the batter and fold them in. With a large metal spoon scoop out one batter-coated plum half and lower it gently into the hot oil. Add another three batter-coated plums to the pan, keeping them separate, then fry for 4–5 minutes, turning the fritters over half-way through. They will expand and set and turn golden brown. Remove with a spider or slotted spoon to kitchen paper to drain. Dredge with caster sugar and serve as soon as possible, frying the remaining fritters in small batches.

**When deep-frying,** strict adherence to a few essential rules will guarantee perfect results. The oil used should be neutral in flavour and capable of sustaining a temperature of 190°C – sealing heat – without burning. Groundnut, rapeseed (canola), sunflower and corn oil are all suitable. Mixed vegetable oils may contain palm oil which is very high in saturated fat. Using clean oil is also very important. Ideally, the contents of a deep-fryer should be changed each time you fry and certainly after no more than three uses. Frying crumbed items degrades the oil fastest.

# Krantz cake

Yeast cakes are a feature of German baking, and this one is filled typically with a walnut and chocolate mixture. It could also have a more spicy, Middle Eastern filling that includes poppy seeds. The recipe was given to Ilan Schwartz by his mother. He cooked it for us when he was head of our *Viennoiserie*.

**MAKES 2 CAKES**

1 SACHET FAST-ACTION YEAST
500G STRONG WHITE FLOUR
1 TABLESPOON WARM BOTTLED
SPRING WATER (ABOUT 20°C)
150G CREAM CHEESE
150G SOUR CREAM
150G CASTER SUGAR
150G UNSALTED BUTTER, MELTED
4 EGG YOLKS
PINCH OF MALDON SALT,
GROUND FINE
SUNFLOWER OIL FOR THE BOWL
AND TINS

**FILLING**
100G CASTER SUGAR
100G WALNUTS
100G GOOD-QUALITY PLAIN
CHOCOLATE

**GLAZE**
1 EGG YOLK
1 TABLESPOON MILK

**SUGAR GLAZE**
50G CASTER SUGAR
50ML BOTTLED SPRING WATER

In a small bowl mix together the yeast, 2 tablespoons of the flour and the warm water. Cover and leave in a warm place for about 2 hours or until the yeast begins to show signs of activity and starts to bubble.

Put the cream cheese, sour cream, sugar, melted butter and egg yolks in the bowl of a heavy-duty electric mixer fitted with the whisk. Whisk together, then add the yeast batter and the remaining flour. Beat on a medium speed for 5–6 minutes, adding the salt as the mixture combines. The dough will be very sticky and difficult to handle. Transfer to a lightly oiled bowl, cover with cling film and leave in the refrigerator overnight.

The next day, remove the dough from the refrigerator 20–30 minutes before you start working with it. Oil two 500g loaf tins.

Make the filling: put the sugar and walnuts in a food processor and blitz to a fine crumb. Transfer to a bowl. Roughly chop the chocolate with a knife, and mix with the sugar and walnuts.

On a lightly floured surface, roll out the dough into a rectangle about 4mm thick. Spread with the filling and roll up like a Swiss roll, starting from a long side. With a sharp knife, cut through the roll lengthways and separate the two pieces. Twist them together loosely, keeping the cut sides up, then cut the twisted loaf across in half. Drop each piece into a prepared loaf tin. Cover with a cloth and leave to rise in a warm place for 1$^1$/$_2$–2 hours or until doubled in bulk.

Preheat the oven to 180°C.

Beat the egg yolk and milk together and brush over the cakes. Bake for 15 minutes, then lower the oven temperature to 160°C and bake for a further 25–30 minutes or until well coloured.

Just before the cakes come out of the oven, make the sugar glaze: dissolve the sugar in the water and bring just to the boil. Brush the hot glaze over the cakes while they are still hot, then leave to cool in the tins for 10 minutes, before turning out on to a wire rack to cool completely.

# QUICK BREADS

'Quick' breads are distinguished by their use of baking powder, bicarbonate of soda and cream of tartar to generate the carbon dioxide which lightens and lifts the loaf instead of yeast. Bicarbonate of soda produces a crisper finish than baking powder. In our recipes we often use a mixture of the two to deliver a perfect texture in a bread, cake or biscuit.

## Cornbread

**Cornbread, made from cornmeal (also called maize meal), is a favourite in the southern states of the USA. Traditionally cornbread is flavoured with bacon fat – the ubiquitous drippings of the Deep South kitchen – but you can substitute butter, lard or olive oil. You can stir various things into the batter to give the bread a different character – crisp pieces of bacon, for example, or fried onions, blanched sweetcorn kernels or, as here, some hot chilli and spring onions.**

SERVES 6

120ML MILK
90G UNSALTED BUTTER + EXTRA FOR THE TIN
240G CORNMEAL
240G PLAIN WHITE FLOUR
2 TEASPOONS BAKING POWDER
2 TEASPOONS BICARBONATE OF SODA
1 TEASPOON MALDON SALT, GROUND FINE
1 EGG
120ML PLAIN LOW-FAT BIO YOGHURT OR BUTTERMILK
1 FRESH GREEN CHILLI, FINELY SHREDDED
2 SPRING ONIONS, THINLY SLICED

Preheat the oven to 180°C. Butter a 20cm round deep cake tin and line the bottom with buttered greaseproof paper.

Warm the milk in a small pan, then remove from the heat and add the butter. Leave to melt off the heat. Sift the dry ingredients into a mixing bowl. Beat the egg with the yoghurt and the buttery milk. Stir in the chilli and spring onions, then fold this mixture into the dry ingredients.

Pour the mixture into the prepared tin. Bake for about 25 minutes or until the top is golden and the bread firm to the touch.

Turn out and cut into wedges while still hot.

**Cornbreads should always be eaten warm** and taste nicest when generously buttered. In the southern states of the USA they are the staple bread, and are eaten with just about every meal. They are particularly good with fried and barbecued foods, such as chicken and spare ribs.

In the Deep South they are traditionally made in heavy iron skillets or frying pans.

Wholemeal soda bread

# White soda bread

Buttermilk – originally the slightly sour residue of milk from which most of the fat has been removed in churning to make butter – is today made commercially from skimmed milk. It gives a rich and distinctive tang to the bread. Health food shops are usually reliable sources of supply, though some supermarkets also stock it. Yoghurt can be substituted.

**MAKES 1 LOAF**

450G PLAIN WHITE FLOUR
1 TEASPOON CASTER SUGAR
1 TEASPOON MALDON SALT, GROUND FINE
1 TEASPOON BICARBONATE OF SODA
1 TEASPOON CREAM OF TARTAR
350ML BUTTERMILK OR THIN PLAIN LOW-FAT BIO YOGHURT

Preheat the oven to 230°C.

Sift the flour into a bowl with the sugar, salt, soda and cream of tartar. Make a well in the centre. Pour in the buttermilk, mixing in with one hand and working from the side of the bowl inwards while turning the bowl with the other hand. The dough should be soft but not too wet and sticky. If it is too dry to hold, add a little more buttermilk.

As soon as it holds, turn out on to a lightly floured surface and knead briefly. Shape into a ball and set on a floured baking tray. Cut a deep cross into the top of the loaf, taking the cuts all the way through to the bottom.

Bake in the middle of the oven for 15 minutes, then turn the oven temperature down to 200°C. Continue to bake for 30 minutes, when the bread should sound hollow when tapped on the base.

# Wholemeal soda bread

An altogether gutsier presentation than the white version, the wheat germ and treacle give this bread a lot of flavour and moistness. It keeps a little better than the white soda bread, but is still best eaten immediately.

Soda bread is a great Irish tradition and should not be thought of as a tea cake. On the contrary, it is excellent with oysters or butter and cheese.

**MAKES 1 LOAF**

300ML BUTTERMILK OR THIN PLAIN LOW-FAT BIO YOGHURT
1 TABLESPOON BLACK TREACLE
220G SELF-RAISING WHITE FLOUR
220G PLAIN WHOLEMEAL FLOUR
1 TABLESPOON WHEAT GERM
$1/2$ TEASPOON CREAM OF TARTAR
1 TEASPOON BICARBONATE OF SODA
1 TEASPOON MALDON SALT, GROUND FINE

Preheat the oven to 190°C.

Warm the buttermilk with the treacle in a small saucepan until the treacle melts. Combine all the dry ingredients in a mixing bowl. Pour over the milk and treacle mixture and mix well with your hands to make a dough. It should be soft but not too wet and sticky.

Shape into a ball and place on a floured baking tray. Cut a deep cross into the top of the loaf, taking the cuts all the way through to the bottom. Bake for 1 hour or until the bread sounds hollow when tapped on the base.

# Scones

The secret of a good moist scone that is also light is in the proportion of raising agent to flour. Use too much leavening and your scone will stand tall, but it will taste horribly of the baking powder chemicals. It is also important to keep the kneading to an absolute minimum or the gluten in the flour gets over-worked, which makes the dough elastic and consequently the baked scone hard.

### MAKES 16 SCONES

450G SELF-RAISING WHITE FLOUR
PINCH OF MALDON SALT,
GROUND FINE
25G CASTER SUGAR + EXTRA FOR
SPRINKLING
2 TEASPOONS BAKING POWDER
85G UNSALTED BUTTER,
SOFTENED
2 EGGS
200ML COLD MILK
85G SULTANAS (OPTIONAL)

### GLAZE
1 EGG YOLK
1 TABLESPOON MILK

Preheat the oven to 150°C. Line a large baking tray with non-stick baking parchment or a silicone mat.

Sift the flour, salt, sugar and baking powder into a bowl. Cut the butter into small cubes and rub into the flour with your hands. Lightly beat the eggs, then add the cold milk. Pour all of the eggy milk mixture into the flour, then mix quickly and lightly together, adding the sultanas if you wish. Do not work the dough too much – the quicker and lighter you are, the better the scones will be.

Tip the dough on to a lightly floured surface and roll out to a thickness of 2.5cm. With an 8cm cutter, cut out 16 rounds and put them 5cm apart on the prepared baking tray.

Lightly beat the egg yolk with the milk for the glaze. Brush over the tops of the scones, then sprinkle with a little caster sugar. Bake in the centre of the oven for 20–25 minutes or until risen and lightly browned. Cool on a wire rack, then split and fill with jam and cream.

## On baking bread

"A loaf can look great and have a good texture, but if it is underseasoned or does not taste right then it is a pointless exercise. There are no short cuts to baking good bread. The process is very complex, with so many variables over which you have no control. For example, you need to take the temperature of the dough coming out of the mixer because if the ambient temperature has pushed it up higher than is desirable then you have to chill the water going into the next batch to compensate.

"Bread is a living thing and you have to love and respect it. Only when you do can your bread move from being good to being remarkable. You must believe in what you are doing. If you do not, there is not enough information in the world to make the magic happen." JASON WARWICK, HEAD BAKER

# Cakes and biscuits

Cakes have from ancient Greek times been both symbolic and special, roles that they continue to play to this day. There are cakes for christenings, wedding celebrations, religious days and festive occasions. The word 'cake' now describes a baked, soft flour-based construction, usually raised with chemical raising agents and invariably sweet. The texture is immediately identifiable as cake and it is distinctively different from bread. This distinction was not always apparent, however, the earliest bread being unleavened and consequently described literally as a cake. The first sweetening of this bread-cake was with honey, but in an age when sweetness did not imply that something should be eaten separately from savoury dishes.

Sweetened yeast breads were probably the first cakes in the modern sense, though the cakes we eat today only started to exist in the last century, with the introduction of baking powders used in conjunction with soft flour batters. Cakes remain treats and culminations. And they are a central part of afternoon tea.

# CAKES

Virtually all cakes are made from soft, low-gluten flour, butter, eggs and sugar, their respective proportions and the method of their incorporation defining the texture of the cake when baked. After that, what makes each cake individual is a matter of shape, flavourings used, and how it is iced, filled and decorated.

The relative proportions of the base ingredients also determine the most appropriate technique to shape a cake's construction. Thus, a high percentage of butter points to 'creaming' at the outset, where the butter is vigorously whipped or whisked with sugar until it becomes pale and absorbs air from the beating action, the air being the element that ensures a light texture when the cake is baked. A cake made with lots of eggs – a classic sponge – begins by whisking them with sugar, and results in a baked finish that literally springs back when gently pressed. Cakes with high levels of treacle, honey or chocolate start

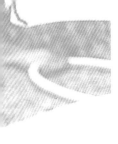

with these being warmed or melted, thereby making it possible to integrate them with the other primary ingredients.

Cake batters are raised using chemicals rather than yeast. The most common raising agents are bicarbonate of soda – which is sometimes referred to as baking soda – and baking powder, of which bicarbonate of soda is the main active ingredient. Chemical raising agents only generate gas briefly, which is why they are unsuitable for lifting breads which need a sustained and lengthy leavening. It is the difference in gluten levels between hard or strong (bread) flours and soft (cake) flours which makes bread and cake texturally so different.

When bicarbonate of soda, an alkali, is mixed with an acid, a chemical reaction is kick-started and carbon dioxide is given off. Bicarbonate of soda can therefore only be used on its own to lift a batter if a suitable natural acid is present. This might be something like lactic acid, which is

contained in yoghurt and buttermilk, or citric acid or vinegar.

Baking powder is a complete raising agent that only needs water to make it work. It consists of a mixture of bicarbonate of soda and acid salts, with ground starch included to absorb moisture from the air. It is this inert 'buffer' of starch that prevents premature activation in the tin in humid conditions.

Baking powder contains two different types of water-soluble salt crystals that are triggered sequentially. The first, typically cream of tartar, reacts with moisture at room temperature and initiates a reaction with the bicarbonate of soda, instantly giving off little bubbles of carbon dioxide. A second acid salt crystal, usually sodium aluminium sulphate, activates only at high temperature, in the oven, generating a larger amount of carbon dioxide. The moist solids of the cake batter dry during cooking and set round the bubbles before

the gas generation stops, producing a light yet moist cake.

Self-raising flour includes baking powder sufficient to raise most cakes, scones and 'quick' breads. (These breads – soda bread and cornbread, for example – which use a chemical raising agent rather than yeast, consequently have a texture more like scone or cake than a yeasted loaf.) However, over years of making cakes at Baker & Spice we have found that many are improved texturally by adding a little bicarbonate of soda or baking powder with the self-raising flour. There is always a trade-off in such experiments, though – add too much and it will leave a bitter chemical taint in the mouth. The cake will also have a tough crumb.

Different brands of self-raising flour contain different amounts of raising agent. The suggested additional raising agent must therefore be treated as a guide and not an absolute.

# Chocolate génoise royale

Génoise cakes are made by a French technique which some people brought up making Victoria sponges initially find tricky. However, an electric mixer helps you achieve a consistent light result easily.

Génoise sponges are best baked the day before they are needed as they will slice better. In fact, they can be refrigerated for up to 3 days or, well wrapped in cling film, may be frozen for 2 weeks without deteriorating. If ever a génoise comes out rather dry, prick the surface deeply with a needle all over and spoon on some rum or brandy, then leave for 12 hours before serving.

This very rich chocolate mousse génoise is based on a recipe developed by our first pastry chef, Henri Berthaux. It makes a fine dessert cake.

### MAKES A 23CM CAKE

#### GÉNOISE
60G UNSALTED BUTTER + EXTRA FOR THE TIN
4 EGGS
115G CASTER SUGAR
115G PLAIN FLOUR
60G COCOA POWDER

#### CHOCOLATE MOUSSE
150G CASTER SUGAR
3 EGGS, SEPARATED + 3 EGG YOLKS
1 TABLESPOON COCOA POWDER
200ML WHIPPING CREAM
100G UNSALTED BUTTER, DICED
250G GOOD-QUALITY BITTERSWEET CHOCOLATE, CHOPPED
1 TABLESPOON BRANDY

#### DECORATION
75G GOOD-QUALITY BITTERSWEET CHOCOLATE, CHOPPED
COCOA POWDER FOR DUSTING

Preheat the oven to 170°C. Butter a 23cm springform cake tin. Line the bottom with a disc of non-stick baking parchment.

Make the génoise: melt the butter in a pan over a low heat. Remove immediately and leave to cool. Put the eggs and sugar into the bowl of a heavy-duty electric mixer fitted with the whisk and beat at a medium speed until the mixture rises. This will take 6–10 minutes. It is very important to incorporate as much air as possible at this stage to ensure a light result. Continue to beat until you achieve a ribbon consistency (1), when the mixture will be quite stiff and an off-white, cream colour.

Remove the bowl from the mixer. Sift the flour and cocoa and add to the bowl. Incorporate by stirring gently (2, 3). Pour in the melted butter and, using a rubber spatula, starting from the centre at the base and working outwards and upwards, fold the mixture over while rotating the bowl one quarter turn (4). Repeat three more times, which means you will have turned the bowl one complete revolution after completing the fourth fold. This is the best way of mixing all the ingredients thoroughly without losing too much air by being heavy-handed – if you overwork the mixture at this point you will end up with a flat and heavy cake.

Pour the mixture into the cake tin, using the spatula to scrape the last of it from the mixing bowl. Put in the oven on the middle rack. Bake for 20 minutes.

Then, working quickly to keep heat loss to a minimum, open the oven door and test that the cake is done by inserting a skewer into the centre. If it comes out clean then it is ready. If sticky crumbs adhere to it, give it another 5 minutes baking and test again. It may possibly still need another 5 minutes. When satisfied it is completely cooked, remove to a wire rack to cool before unmoulding.

*continued overleaf*

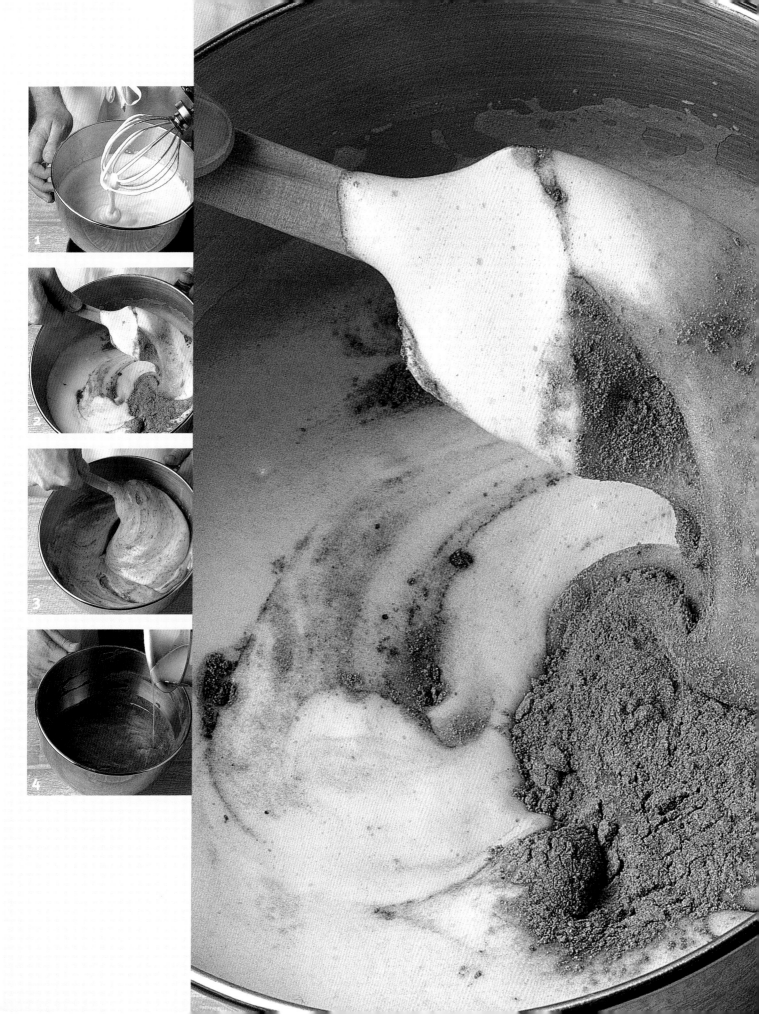

Carefully slice off the risen centre of the cake to give a flat surface. Wash and dry the springform tin. Cut a strip of non-stick baking parchment to fit around the inside of the tin. Put the prepared génoise back in and reserve.

To make the chocolate mousse, put 50g of the sugar, the 6 egg yolks, cocoa powder and the cream in a bowl set over a pan of simmering water. Stir with a wooden spoon until hot, or the mixture thickens sufficiently to coat the back of the spoon. (If confident, you can make the custard in a saucepan over a low heat, which has the benefit of being much quicker.) Remove from the heat and gradually beat in the butter and chocolate until melted and fully combined. Stir in the brandy. Whisk the egg whites with the remaining sugar to soft peaks, then fold them into the mixture.

Pour the mousse mixture on top of the génoise base in the tin. Cover and refrigerate for 4 hours or overnight before unmoulding.

When ready to serve, unmould carefully by sliding a warm palette knife round the inside of the tin before unclipping the side. Leave the cake on the tin base.

For the decoration, melt the chocolate in a bowl set over a pan of just simmering water. Pour on to a clean, dry metal tray and spread out thinly. As the chocolate cools, test it every so often – you want to catch it before it sets hard. When the chocolate is firm enough to work with, shave off large curls using a palette knife. Transfer the curls carefully to the top of the cake, piling them up. Finish with a dusting of cocoa powder.

For a plain génoise, just omit the cocoa powder. A slice of plain génoise with seasonal berries or a fruit coulis makes a light and elegant dessert.

# Chocolate pecan cake

The all-American pecan nut, indigenous to Louisiana and nearby places, shares with walnuts a rich taste and a two-lobed appearance. Pecans also have a similar propensity for going rancid really fast, so they must be used up quickly. Don't freeze them because when thawed they go odd very quickly.

The combination of chocolate and pecans in this cake is pleasing, not overly sweet like pecan pie so often is. The cake is very rich and buttery, however, and a small slice satisfies.

**MAKES A 23CM CAKE**

180G GOOD-QUALITY BITTERSWEET CHOCOLATE, CHOPPED
180G UNSALTED BUTTER + EXTRA FOR THE TIN
4 EGGS, SEPARATED
140G CASTER SUGAR
225G PECAN NUTS, GROUND
100G PLAIN FLOUR, SIFTED

**ICING**
360G GOOD-QUALITY BITTERSWEET CHOCOLATE, CHOPPED
250G UNSALTED BUTTER
2 TABLESPOONS GOLDEN SYRUP

**DECORATION**
50G WHITE CHOCOLATE, CHOPPED

Preheat the oven to 180°C. Butter a 23cm springform cake tin. Line the bottom with a disc of non-stick baking parchment.

Make the cake: melt the chocolate and butter in a heavy-based pan over a low heat, then set aside to cool. Put the egg yolks and two-thirds of the sugar in the bowl of a heavy-duty electric mixer fitted with the whisk and beat until thick and light in colour. In another bowl, whisk the egg whites with the remaining sugar until they will hold a firm peak. Fold the melted chocolate into the whisked egg yolks, then fold in the ground pecans and flour. Finally, fold in the whisked egg whites.

Pour the cake mixture into the tin. Bake in the centre of the oven for 45–50 minutes or until a skewer inserted into the centre of the cake comes out with a few slightly sticky crumbs clinging to it. Transfer to a wire rack and leave to cool completely in the tin.

To make the icing, combine the chocolate, butter and golden syrup in a heavy-based pan and warm over a low flame until smoothly combined. Remove from the heat and leave to cool to a thick, pouring consistency before using.

Remove the cake from the tin and place it on a rack set over a tray. Pour over the icing, spreading it gently over the top and sides with a palette knife.

For the decoration, melt the white chocolate in a bowl set over a pan of just simmering water. Put into a small greaseproof paper piping cone (or a small polythene bag), snip off the tip and pipe in random lines over the chocolate icing on the top of the cake. Draw a skewer through the piped white icing to make squiggles. Leave to set before serving.

## On cakes

"What makes a cake special are the quality of the ingredients, their generosity and their freshness, not elaborate decoration. Our cakes are essentially simple constructions that are complete when they come from the oven. They are closer to good home baking than classic French pâtisserie, with its complex creams, additives and custards. You don't have to have 20 stages to make something delicious.

"Small changes in the balance of ingredients can make big changes in the finished cake. There are no revolutions – things are made better very gradually, a natural process that takes time. This is the same as at home when a recipe is cooked over and over, with little changes and refinements each time." DORIT MAINZER, PASTRY COOK

# Coffee cake with mascarpone cream

This recipe was given to us by David Whitehouse, whose pâtisserie, Leamingtons of Richmond, sadly had to close — like so many of the better high street English bakers. The pronounced coffee flavour in the cake provides the perfect balance for the rich mascarpone filling. Unusually for an English cake, the fat used is corn oil.

**MAKES A 20CM CAKE WITH 2 TIERS**

225G SELF-RAISING FLOUR
2 TEASPOONS BAKING POWDER
225G CASTER SUGAR
225ML CORN OIL
2 EGGS, SEPARATED
4 TEASPOONS COFFEE EXTRACT, OR 2 HEAPED TEASPOONS INSTANT COFFEE GRANULES DISSOLVED IN 2 TEASPOONS BOILING WATER
75ML FULL-FAT MILK
BUTTER FOR THE TIN

**ICING**

250G MASCARPONE
1/4 TEASPOON GRATED LEMON ZEST
350G ICING SUGAR, SIFTED
2 TABLESPOONS STRONG ESPRESSO, OR 2 HEAPED TEASPOONS INSTANT ESPRESSO DISSOLVED IN 2 TABLESPOONS BOILING WATER

Preheat the oven to 180°C. Butter two 20cm springform cake tins and line the bottom of each with a disc of non-stick baking parchment.

Sift the flour, baking powder and caster sugar into a mixing bowl. Beat in the oil, egg yolks, coffee and milk. In a second bowl, whisk the egg whites to soft peaks. Stir a spoonful of the whites into the cake mixture before gently folding the rest through. Divide the mixture equally between the tins. Bake for about 45 minutes or until the sponges spring back when gently pressed in the centre. Transfer to a rack to cool, unmoulding the cakes while still warm and leaving them on the rack to cool completely.

For the mascarpone icing, put the mascarpone and lemon zest in a bowl and mix together with a spoon. Slowly add the icing sugar, about one-third at a time, working each addition in completely with the spoon before adding the next until you have a thick paste. Finally, beat in the coffee, a spoonful at a time, until completely incorporated.

Spread half the icing on one sponge, then put the second sponge on top. Smooth the remainder of the icing over the top of the cake using a palette knife.

# Honey and spice cake

The very loose cake mixture here delivers a light and airy result. Unusually, a little fresh ginger juice spikes the mixture, underpinning the more aromatic ground spices with its clean, hot taste.

**MAKES 1 LARGE LOAF CAKE**

3CM PIECE OF FRESH ROOT GINGER, PEELED
125G RUNNY HONEY
50G GOLDEN SYRUP
140G UNSALTED BUTTER
50G DARK SOFT BROWN SUGAR
2 EGGS
40G RYE FLOUR
100G SELF-RAISING FLOUR
1/2 TEASPOON BAKING POWDER
1/2 TEASPOON GROUND CINNAMON
1/2 TEASPOON GROUND ALLSPICE

Grate the ginger on to a double thickness of muslin. Holding the muslin over a bowl, wind it round the ginger like a spring to squeeze out as much juice as you can. Discard the ginger pulp. Reserve the juice.

Preheat the oven to 170°C. Line the bottom and sides of a 1kg loaf tin with non-stick baking parchment.

In a saucepan over a low heat, warm the honey, golden syrup, butter and brown sugar until hot and the butter is almost melted. Transfer the mixture to the bowl of a heavy-duty electric mixer fitted with the whisk. Beat for 2¹/₂ minutes at medium speed, then add the eggs and ginger juice and continue beating for another 2¹/₂ minutes. The mixture will have cooled, lightened with the air beaten into it and thickened appreciably.

Sift together the flours, baking powder and ground spices, then sift a second time. Fold the dry ingredients into the honey mixture using a spatula. The mixture will be unusually wet. Pour it into the tin and set on a baking tray in the centre of the oven. Bake for 50–60 minutes or until the top of the cake is a dark golden brown and it feels spongy, springing back lightly when gently pressed.

Transfer to a rack and leave to cool to room temperature in the tin before unmoulding.

# Marble cake

Swirling the chocolate through the batter gives the cake its distinctive appearance when cut and hence the name. This effect is best achieved by dividing the mixture between two bowls, only adding the chocolate to one of them. The cake is then built with alternate spoonfuls.

**MAKES 1 LARGE LOAF CAKE**

100G GOOD-QUALITY BITTERSWEET CHOCOLATE, CHOPPED
125ML MILK
120G UNSALTED BUTTER, SOFTENED
170G CASTER SUGAR
2 EGGS
225G SELF-RAISING FLOUR
1 TEASPOON BAKING POWDER
65G SOUR CREAM
BUTTER AND FLOUR FOR THE TIN

Preheat the oven to 170°C. Lightly grease a 1kg loaf tin with melted butter. Cut a rectangle of non-stick baking parchment to fit the bottom of the tin and put it in place. Butter the paper, then dust the paper and the inside of the tin with a little flour.

Put the chocolate and 50ml of the milk in a bowl and set over simmering water to melt. Remove from the heat.

In a heavy-duty electric mixer, cream the butter with the sugar until light in colour and fluffy in texture. Slowly beat in the eggs, one at a time, until well combined. Sift the flour with the baking powder. Mix together the sour cream and remaining milk. Fold a third of the flour into the butter and egg mixture, followed by a third of the sour cream mixture. Fold another third of the flour into the mixture, again with a third of the sour cream. Fold in the remaining flour and sour cream. Spoon half of the mixture into another bowl. Add the chocolate mixture to one half and fold in.

**Honey and spice cake, top, and Marble cake**

Spoon the two mixtures into the tin, taking it alternately from the bowls to give a marbled effect. Set the tin on a baking tray in the middle of the oven and bake for 50–55 minutes or until a skewer inserted in the centre of the cake comes out clean.

Leave to cool in the tin for 10 minutes, then run a knife between the cake and the sides of the tin. Very gently upturn the cake on to your cloth-covered hand, then place upright on a wire rack to finish cooling.

Lemon cake

# Lemon cake

**Light yet full of flavour, this is a fresh-tasting sponge cake with an appealing and strong citrus colour.**

**MAKES 1 SMALL LOAF CAKE**

115G SELF-RAISING FLOUR
1 TEASPOON BAKING POWDER
2 EGGS
115G CASTER SUGAR
65ML DOUBLE CREAM
GRATED ZEST OF 1 LEMON
1 TABLESPOON LEMON JUICE
45G UNSALTED BUTTER, MELTED
BUTTER AND FLOUR FOR
THE TIN

**ICING**

30G ICING SUGAR
1 TEASPOON LEMON JUICE

Preheat the oven to 170°C. Lightly grease a 500g loaf tin with melted butter. Cut a rectangle of non-stick baking parchment to cover the bottom of the tin. Put the paper in place and butter it, then dust the paper and side of the tin with a little flour.

Sift together the flour and baking powder. Lightly beat the eggs with the sugar until just combined. Beat the cream into the eggs for a minute, then add the lemon zest and juice. Fold in the flour until lightly combined, then gently and carefully fold in the melted butter.

Pour the mixture into the loaf tin. Set the tin on a baking tray in the middle of the oven and bake for 45 minutes or until a skewer inserted in the centre of the cake comes out clean. Leave to cool in the tin for 10 minutes, then run a knife between the cake and the sides of the tin. Very gently upturn the cake on to your cloth-covered hand, then place the cake upright on a wire rack to finish cooling.

To make the icing, sift the icing sugar into a small bowl. Slowly add two-thirds of the lemon juice, stirring until combined. Add more lemon juice to make a slightly thin icing, but be careful not to thin it too much – the icing will thin further when left for 2–3 minutes.

Brush the icing over the top of the cake, letting it drip a little down the sides.

# Apricot cake

**A rich batter produces a classic sponge, the apricots on the top nestling in the cake which rises up around them as it bakes. Semi-ripe, firm plums can be used instead of apricots.**

**MAKES A 23CM CAKE**

200G UNSALTED BUTTER,
SOFTENED
350G CASTER SUGAR
3 EGGS
225G SELF-RAISING FLOUR
150G SOUR CREAM
12 APRICOTS, CUT IN HALF AND
STONE REMOVED
BUTTER AND FLOUR FOR THE TIN

**TO FINISH**

45G CASTER SUGAR

Preheat the oven to 170°C. Lightly grease a 23cm springform cake tin with melted butter. Line the bottom with a disc of non-stick baking parchment and butter it, then dust the paper and the side of the tin with a little flour.

In a heavy-duty electric mixer, cream the butter with the sugar until light and fluffy. Slowly beat in the eggs, one at a time, until well combined. Fold a third of the flour into the butter and egg mixture, followed by a third of the sour cream. Then fold in another third of the flour and sour cream. Finally, fold in the remaining flour and sour cream.

Spoon the mixture into the prepared cake tin. Lay the fruit on the surface, cut side up, leaning each apricot half slightly on to the next in concentric circles to cover the top completely. Finish by sprinkling with the extra sugar. Bake in the centre of the oven for 50 minutes or until a skewer inserted into the centre of the cake comes out clean.

Leave to cool in the tin for 10 minutes, then run a knife between the cake and the side of the tin. Release the spring-lock on the side of the tin, remove the collar and leave the cake to cool completely on a rack.

# Carrot cake

An American classic, carrot cake is unusual both in its use of a root vegetable in an otherwise very sweet construction and in using oil for the fat content rather than the more typical butter or margarine. The predominant flavour is of cinnamon, its potential stridency moderated by backnotes of nutmeg and cloves, the overall sweetness of the cake nicely balanced by the highly aromatic spicing. The cake's texture is made unusually moist by the carrots.

**MAKES A 23CM CAKE WITH 2 TIERS**

300G SELF-RAISING FLOUR
1/4 TEASPOON BAKING POWDER
1/4 TEASPOON BICARBONATE OF SODA
1 TEASPOON GROUND CINNAMON
1/2 TEASPOON GROUND CLOVES
1/4 TEASPOON GRATED NUTMEG
PINCH OF MALDON SALT, GROUND FINE
4 EGGS
335ML SUNFLOWER OIL
450G CASTER SUGAR
125G GRATED CARROTS
140G CHOPPED WALNUTS
2 TABLESPOONS HOT BOTTLED SPRING WATER
BUTTER AND FLOUR FOR THE TIN

**ICING**

130G UNSALTED BUTTER, SOFTENED
300G FULL-FAT SOFT CHEESE (PHILADELPHIA), SOFTENED
160G ICING SUGAR, SIFTED

Preheat the oven to 180°C. Lightly grease two 23cm springform cake tins with melted butter. Line the bottom of each tin with a disc of non-stick baking parchment. Butter the paper, then dust the paper and the side of the tins with a little flour.

Sift together the flour, baking powder, bicarbonate of soda, spices and salt. Separate 2 of the eggs.

In the bowl of a heavy-duty electric mixer, beat together the oil and the sugar. Slowly add the whole eggs, beating well, then beat in the 2 egg yolks. Beat in the grated carrots, then stir in the chopped walnuts. Fold in the sifted flour followed by the hot water. In another bowl, whisk the 2 egg whites until soft peaks form. Fold them into the batter.

Divide the cake mixture between the prepared tins. Set the tins on a baking tray in the middle of the oven and bake for 45 minutes or until a skewer inserted into the centre of a cake comes out clean. Leave to cool in the tins for 10 minutes, then run a knife between the cakes and the sides of the tin. Release the spring-lock, remove the collar and leave the cakes to cool on a rack.

To make the icing, beat all the ingredients together to a thick cream. With a palette knife, spread a layer of icing on one cake, then press the other on top. Spread the rest of the icing over the top and side of the cake, swirling it attractively. Refrigerate for at least 2 hours before serving, and keep in the fridge as the icing will soften at room temperature.

# Devil's food cake

Cakes bearing this rather provocative title, with all its implications of wicked excess, are often disappointing, typically being too sweet and not chocolatey enough. Our Devil's cake uses an unusually large amount of melted chocolate, both in the sponge and in the icing, to strike the right indulgent note.

**MAKES A 23CM CAKE
WITH 4 TIERS**

150G GOOD-QUALITY
BITTERSWEET CHOCOLATE,
CHOPPED
115G CASTER SUGAR
125ML MILK
40G COCOA POWDER
3 EGGS, SEPARATED + 1 EGG
YOLK
150G UNSALTED BUTTER,
SOFTENED + EXTRA FOR
THE TIN
85G MUSCOVADO SUGAR
225G PLAIN FLOUR
1 TEASPOON MALDON SALT,
GROUND FINE
1 TEASPOON BICARBONATE OF
SODA
170G SOUR CREAM

**ICING**
200G GOOD-QUALITY
BITTERSWEET CHOCOLATE,
CHOPPED
60G COCOA POWDER
100ML BOTTLED SPRING WATER
1 TABLESPOON GOLDEN SYRUP
45G UNSALTED BUTTER,
SOFTENED
280G ICING SUGAR, SIFTED
2 EGG YOLKS

Preheat the oven to 170°C. Butter two 23cm springform cake tins and line the bottom of each with a disc of non-stick baking parchment.

Make the cake: put the chocolate, caster sugar, milk, cocoa powder and 2 egg yolks in a bowl set over simmering water. Stir to make a coherent custard-like mixture. Remove from the pan of water and reserve.

In the bowl of a heavy-duty electric mixer, beat the butter with the muscovado sugar until light and fluffy. Beat in the remaining 2 egg yolks, then the flour, salt and bicarbonate of soda. Fold in the sour cream followed by the chocolate mixture. In another bowl, whisk the egg whites until they hold firm peaks, then fold through the cake mixture until combined.

Divide the mixture between the tins and lightly smooth the top. Bake in the centre of the oven for 45–50 minutes or until a skewer inserted into a cake comes out clean. Transfer to a rack and leave to cool completely in the tins.

To make the icing, put the chocolate in a bowl and set over simmering water to melt. In a pan over a low heat, warm the cocoa powder, water and golden syrup until hot but not boiling. Add the melted chocolate and whisk until combined. Remove from the heat and beat in the butter, icing sugar and egg yolks until smooth and creamy. Taste and add a little more sugar if liked. Leave to cool until the icing is thick but spreadable.

Remove the cakes from the tins and cut each into two layers. Sandwich the four layers together, spreading a little icing between them, and finish by icing the top and side of the cake thickly, spreading the icing with a palette knife. Leave in a cool place overnight to firm, but not in the refrigerator which would make the icing go dull.

# Blueberry bran muffins

The muffin's popularity in Britain goes from strength to strength, though people do not yet make them very much at home. This may be because you need to buy a muffin tray in which to cook them, though the muffins can also be baked in doubled paper cake cases. Muffin tins usually have 12 cups which should be at least 6.5cm deep. When baked, the muffins should have a firm texture, unlike a sponge, the top well risen and golden brown. Often the crown splits slightly which is how it should be.

Eat the muffins warm – they are never as nice when completely cold.

**MAKES 18 MUFFINS**

100G BRAN
300ML MILK
300G SELF-RAISING WHITE FLOUR
2 TEASPOONS BICARBONATE OF SODA
1 TEASPOON BAKING POWDER
3 EGGS
160G CASTER SUGAR
85G MUSCOVADO SUGAR
300ML SUNFLOWER OIL + EXTRA FOR THE TRAY
200G BLUEBERRIES, WASHED AND LEFT TO DRY

Preheat the oven to 170°C. Lightly oil the cups in the muffin tray.

Mix the bran and milk together. Leave aside until you have mixed the other ingredients. Sift the flour, bicarbonate of soda and baking powder together. In a large bowl, lightly beat the eggs with the sugars and oil. Fold in the sifted flour, then lightly fold in the soaked bran and milk. Finally, add the fruit and fold lightly to combine. Do not overmix – there should still be some traces of flour evident.

Spoon the mixture into the muffin cups to fill almost to the top. Bake in the centre of the oven for 20–25 minutes. Leave to cool until warm, then eat immediately.

# Chocolate and hazelnut brownies

Chocolate brownies probably owe their popularity to their rich and moist interior, which conjures up childhood memories of the joys of uncooked cake batters. To ensure the right consistency, the batter should be worked gently – beating hard will incorporate too much air, delivering a spongy finish.

**MAKES 16 SQUARE BROWNIES**

120G UNSALTED BUTTER, SOFTENED
250G CASTER SUGAR
2 EGGS + 1 EGG YOLK
210G GOOD-QUALITY
BITTERSWEET CHOCOLATE,
MELTED
4 TABLESPOONS ESPRESSO
1 TABLESPOON RUM OR BRANDY
165G PLAIN FLOUR
1 TEASPOON BAKING POWDER
1/4 TEASPOON MALDON SALT,
GROUND FINE
WHOLE HAZELNUTS
ICING SUGAR FOR SPRINKLING

Preheat the oven to 180°C. Cut a piece of foil to cover the bottom and sides of a 23cm square tin that is 5cm deep.

Cream the butter with the sugar. Slowly add the eggs, one at a time, and then the yolk, mixing well after each addition. Stir in the melted chocolate, then the coffee and the rum (or brandy). Sift the flour, baking powder and salt together, and gently fold into the chocolate mix.

Pour into the tin. Gently press some whole hazelnuts over the surface. Bake in the middle of the oven for 20–25 minutes: a skewer inserted near the centre of the cake should come out warm at the tip and with slightly sticky crumbs clinging to it. (The greatest danger when baking brownies is overcooking, which turns them into dry chocolate sponges. It is therefore better to err on the side of underdone.)

Leave to cool in the tin before cutting into squares and dusting with icing sugar.

# Orange cheesecake brownies

A rippled effect is achieved by piping and swirling in a sweet cheese mixture and sandwiching it between layers of sticky chocolate. The contrast of flavour and texture is very appealing.

**MAKES 16 SQUARE BROWNIES**

340G FULL-FAT SOFT CHEESE,
SOFTENED
100G CASTER SUGAR
1 EGG YOLK
30G PLAIN FLOUR
GRATED ZEST OF 1 ORANGE
1 TABLESPOON FRESHLY
SQUEEZED ORANGE JUICE
1 RECIPE CHOCOLATE BROWNIES
MIXTURE (SEE ABOVE)

Preheat the oven to 180°C. Cut a piece of foil to cover the bottom and sides of a 23cm square tin that is 5cm deep.

Cream together the soft cheese and sugar. Add the egg yolk, followed by the flour. Finish by mixing in the orange zest and juice. It is important that the consistency be quite thick: achieving a similar texture between the cheese and the chocolate brownies mixtures will make swirling the cheese mixture into the chocolate base easier. Put the cheese mixture into a piping bag fitted with a 1cm nozzle.

Spoon half of the brownie mixture into the tin. Pipe half of the cheese over the top, moving from one side to another in swirling bands, pushing the cheese into the chocolate mixture as you do so. Spoon on half of the remaining brownie mixture, then pipe over the remaining cheese, pushing it into the chocolate as before. Finish by spooning on the last of the chocolate. Take a skewer and zig-zag the swirls to accentuate the effect.

Bake as for Chocolate and hazelnut brownies.

# BISCUITS AND COOKIES

Biscuits and cookies are delicious fripperies, never the main event perhaps, but simple constructions which at their most delicate can please a discerning palate. In their sugary and more accessible forms they have given pleasure to children and the young-at-heart since medieval times, sweet mouthfuls that crunch appealingly and then burst with candied flavour on the tongue.

Biscuits to the British are cookies to Americans, and both terms describe a huge variety of sweet or sometimes savoury bites that are usually – but not invariably – small, crisp discs or wafers. They may be lightly leavened – a small sponge can sometimes be a biscuit – and their texture can be soft or chewy like toffee or snapping-crisp. They may be tooth-achingly sweet with sugar or honey or, by contrast, be salty or flavoured with cheese or anchovies (when Americans would more likely call them crackers).

Chocolate biscuits can be dry with just a hint of chocolate or moist, spongy and

intensely chocolate flavoured. Rich biscuits are shortened with masses of butter, while a water biscuit makes a dry and austere partner for cheese. Dried fruit can outweigh the crumb in a recipe, but it does not stop the end result from being called a biscuit. Meringues are biscuits too, as are fig rolls, Garibaldis, shortbread, cream crackers, rusks, cheese straws, ginger nuts, chocolate chip cookies, sugar-crusted langues-de-chat and almond tuiles.

The first biscuits were not unlike the first breads, crude and coarse flat cakes bound with water and cooked on a griddle. Oat cakes were probably one of the first biscuits ever made. With the wider availability of wheat, simple water and flour biscuits became standard fare for travellers. Slow-baked twice to eliminate all moisture, this was the hard tack which sustained the early sailors, so hard it had to be soaked in water before it could be chewed. It also had to be tough enough to resist infestation by

insects, at least for several months – after a year at sea, ship's biscuits seethed with weevils. The first biscuits baked for culinary pleasure were served after medieval banquets and often literally contained sweetened fish and meats along with the sugar and spices that proclaimed a person's wealth and generosity to the world.

By the 1600s sweet biscuits were widely eaten in well-to-do households, typically little pieces of sweet pastry coated with sugar icing, though not all biscuits were sweet. The Bath Oliver was the eighteenth century invention of a certain Dr Oliver of Bath who claimed great digestive properties for them. He encouraged his society patients to eat them as a remedy to counter the effects of their meat-rich diet, an eighteenth-century pointer towards a later scientific understanding of balanced diet and nutrition.

Biscuits gradually developed national or cultural chracteristics which are still

identifiable today. Thin wafers perfumed with rose or orange water and studded with slivered nuts are popular in the Middle East and North Africa, while rye and poppy seed crispbreads are very Scandinavian. American cookies still celebrate New World ingredients such as chocolate, pecan nuts and molasses. Biscuits based on a stiff dough that can be cut in any shape often have attachments to religious festivals, some dating back to a pre-Christian era. One thinks of gingerbread men and the German Christmas *springerle* — glazed biscuits with animal figures representing the Nativity, which are punched from a specially embossed rolling pin.

# Shortbread

Shortbread is so called because of its high fat content, short being the abbreviation of shortening which in this rich, crumbly biscuit means butter. At Baker & Spice we bake our shortbread in a rectangular tin, to be cut into bars, but if you prefer, bake it in traditional rounds.

**MAKES 16 BARS OR 10–12 WEDGES**

150G UNSALTED BUTTER + EXTRA FOR THE TIN
225G PLAIN FLOUR
4 TABLESPOONS CORNFLOUR
1/2 TEASPOON BAKING POWDER
125G CASTER SUGAR + EXTRA FOR SPRINKLING
1/4 TEASPOON MALDON SALT, GROUND FINE
1 TEASPOON VANILLA ESSENCE (OPTIONAL)

Lightly butter a 24 x 20cm Swiss roll tin (or two 16cm fluted tart tins).

Dice the butter straight from the fridge and put into a mixing bowl to soften for about 30 minutes. Sift the flour, cornflour and baking powder on top, then add the sugar and salt. (If using, the vanilla essence can be added now.) Rub together gently between your fingertips and, as the mixture coheres, form it into a ball. Alternatively, put the sifted flour, cornflour, baking powder, salt and sugar in the bowl of a heavy-duty electric mixer fitted with the whisk. Add the diced butter, then turn the machine on at low speed and mix until the butter and flour have combined and the mixture resembles breadcrumbs.

For bars, gently pack the mixture into the Swiss roll tin. Incise the surface to mark out bars, cutting lengthways in half and then across. Prick the top all over with a fork.

For a traditional presentation, shake some caster sugar on to a work surface, put the dough on to it and cut in half, shaping into two equal balls. Put each ball into a tart tin and gently press out into an even layer, making it slightly thicker at the edges and crimping between finger and thumb. Prick the surface all over with a fork and incise 4 bisecting shallow cuts from edge to edge like the spokes of a wheel so that the biscuit can be divided neatly into 8 equal wedges when baked.

Refrigerate for 30 minutes to 1 hour, then preheat the oven to 180°C. Bake for 18–20 minutes, when the surface will be slightly coloured and just firm to the touch. Leave in the tins until completely cooled before removing.

# Benedict bar

Shortbread lends itself to a number of rich toppings. This one is reminiscent of Bakewell tart. It is called Benedict bar, because it is similar to the South African Benedict cake. The idea came from Jeanne Hertz, who was a member of our talented pâtisserie team.

**MAKES 16 BARS**

100G UNSALTED BUTTER
60G CASTER SUGAR
1 TEASPOON VANILLA ESSENCE
200G FLAKED ALMONDS
3 TABLESPOONS MILK
1 RECIPE SHORTBREAD DOUGH (SEE ABOVE)
RASPBERRY JAM

Preheat the oven to 180°C. Lightly butter a 24 x 20cm Swiss roll tin.

Put the butter, sugar, vanilla essence, almonds and milk in a small, heavy-based saucepan over the lowest heat, and warm until the butter has melted. Remove from the heat and leave until cool.

Press the shortbread dough into the tin. Spread a thin layer of jam over the surface, then spread the topping mixture over the jam. Bake as for Shortbread, allowing 25–30 minutes.

Benedict bar

# Date shortbread bars

**Chewy, sweet and aromatic, the date filling with its citrus tang of orange and smoky cinnamon contrasts nicely with the crisp and buttery biscuit.**

**MAKES 16 BARS**

250G DATES
GRATED ZEST OF 1 ORANGE
25G UNSALTED BUTTER + EXTRA
FOR THE TIN
1 TEASPOON GROUND CINNAMON
200ML BOTTLED SPRING WATER
1 RECIPE SHORTBREAD DOUGH
(PAGE 116)

Preheat the oven to 180°C. Lightly butter a 24 x 20cm Swiss roll tin.

Put the dates, orange zest, butter, cinnamon and water in a pan and bring to the boil. Remove from the heat and leave to cool before putting the mixture in a food processor. Pulse-chop to a coarse paste and use at once.

Press two-thirds of the shortbread dough into the tin. Spread the date topping mixture over the surface. Sprinkle the remaining shortbread dough on top like a crumble. Bake for 25–30 minutes. Leave to cool in the tin.

# Chocolate biscuits

With an exquisitely crisp exterior and a contrasting soft, chewy centre made from a blend of the finest dark and bitter chocolates, these elegant biscuits crunch when bitten, then melt in the mouth.

**MAKES 20–30 BISCUITS**

110G PLAIN FLOUR
30G COCOA POWDER
1 TEASPOON BICARBONATE OF SODA
1/2 TEASPOON MALDON SALT, GROUND FINE
115G GOOD-QUALITY BITTERSWEET CHOCOLATE
50G GOOD-QUALITY BITTER CHOCOLATE, SUCH AS VALHRONA GRAND CARAQUE
80G UNSALTED BUTTER, SOFTENED + EXTRA FOR THE TRAYS
175G LIGHT SOFT BROWN SUGAR
1 EGG

Sift together the flour, cocoa powder, soda and salt. Melt the chocolates together in a bowl set over simmering water, then leave to cool.

In a heavy-duty electric mixer, cream the butter with the sugar, whisking at high speed until pale and creamy. Slowly add the egg and beat until combined. Fold in the sifted flour and cocoa mixture, then fold in the melted chocolate. Cover and leave to rest in the refrigerator for 1 hour.

Preheat the oven to 180°C.

Roll the dough into egg-sized pieces between your palms and place on buttered baking trays, leaving space for them to spread as they cook. Press them down slightly with your fingers to flatten. Bake for 15–20 minutes or until the edges are firm, but the centre still will give a little to the touch. Leave to cool on the trays for a minute, then remove to a wire rack to cool completely.

Eat immediately or store in an airtight tin or cookie jar for up to 5 days.

# Oatmeal and raisin cookies

Moist, sweet and definitely more-ish, these oatmeal and raisin cookies are enjoyed by adults and children alike. For a more sophisticated flavour, soak the raisins in brandy for a couple of hours before incorporating them in the dough.

**MAKES 20 COOKIES**

115G UNSALTED BUTTER, SOFTENED
100G LIGHT SOFT BROWN SUGAR
115G CASTER SUGAR
1 EGG, LIGHTLY BEATEN
4 TABLESPOONS BOTTLED SPRING WATER
2 TEASPOONS VANILLA ESSENCE
100G SELF-RAISING FLOUR
1 TEASPOON MALDON SALT, GROUND FINE
250G ROLLED OATS
100G SULTANAS

Preheat the oven to 180°C. Line two baking trays with non-stick baking parchment.

In a heavy-duty electric mixer, cream the butter with the sugars until light and fluffy. Gradually add the egg, beating until evenly combined. Then beat in the water and the vanilla essence before folding in the remaining ingredients.

Roll the dough into walnut-sized pieces between your palms and put them on the baking trays, leaving space between the cookies to allow for expansion as they cook. Bake for 15 minutes or until firm but still with some give to the gentle press of a finger. Leave to cool on the trays for a few minutes before transferring to a wire rack.

# Chocolate chip cookies

The chocolate chip cookie was created by accident and we know precisely when, where and by whom. In 1933, Ruth Wakefield, who owned the Toll House Inn in Whitman, Massachusetts, added chocolate chips to a cookie batter, assuming they would melt and merge during baking to produce a uniformly textured chocolate-flavoured wafer. Instead the pieces of chocolate stayed moistly intact, and the chocolate chip cookie was born.

The Baker & Spice version of this American institution is intensely flavoured, rich and chewy. They are appreciated by Baker & Spice's many US expatriate customers, who say the cookies make them nostalgic for home. We use ready-made chocolate chips, but you can cut small pieces from a block of good-quality chocolate if you prefer.

**MAKES ABOUT 30 COOKIES**

160G UNSALTED BUTTER, SOFTENED + EXTRA FOR THE TRAYS
85G LIGHT SOFT BROWN SUGAR
85G CASTER SUGAR
2 EGGS
400G PLAIN FLOUR
1/2 TEASPOON BICARBONATE OF SODA
1/2 TEASPOON BAKING POWDER
1/4 TEASPOON MALDON SALT, GROUND FINE
200G SEMI-SWEET CHOCOLATE PIECES, OR 200G GOOD-QUALITY BITTERSWEET CHOCOLATE, CUT INTO SMALL CHUNKS

Preheat the oven to 180°C.

In the bowl of a heavy-duty electric mixer fitted with the whisk, cream the butter with the sugars until light and fluffy. Add the eggs, one at a time, waiting until the first is completely incorporated before adding the second to avoid the mixture splitting. Sift together the flour, bicarbonate of soda, baking powder and salt, then fold into the mixture, followed by the chocolate chips, using a spatula. You will have a stiff dough.

Roll walnut-sized pieces of dough between your palms and put them on two buttered baking trays, leaving space between the cookies to allow for expansion as they cook. Bake for 15–20 minutes or until the edges are firm but the centre still has some give to the gentle press of a finger.

Remove and leave to cool on the trays for a minute before transferring to a wire rack to cool to room temperature. Eat immediately or store in an airtight tin or cookie jar for up to 5 days.

(Opposite) Oatmeal and raisin cookies on plate and Chocolate chip cookies in glass jar

# Pecan butter cookies

The butter really is the defining ingredient in these cookies, and its quality makes all the difference. Seek out a really good Normandy butter. It will make the cookies memorable.

**MAKES ABOUT 30 COOKIES**

350G PLAIN FLOUR
PINCH OF MALDON SALT, GROUND FINE
300G UNSALTED BUTTER, SOFTENED
60G CASTER SUGAR
140G PECAN NUTS, COARSELY CHOPPED
ICING SUGAR FOR DUSTING

Preheat the oven to 180°C. Line two baking trays with non-stick baking parchment.

Sift together the flour and salt. Cream the butter with the sugar until light in colour and texture. Beat in the chopped pecans, then fold in the flour.

Roll walnut-sized pieces of dough between your palms and put them on the baking trays, leaving space between the cookies to allow for expansion as they cook. Flatten them a little with your fingers. Bake for 15–20 minutes or until firm but still with some give to the gentle press of a finger. Cool on the baking trays for a few minutes before transferring to a wire rack. Toss in icing sugar while still warm.

# Lemon butter cookies

The pronounced lemon flavour balances the butter richness to perfection in these beautiful amber discs, which bake to a golden crisp at the rim.

**MAKES 30–36 COOKIES**

115G CASTER SUGAR
GRATED ZEST OF 2 LEMONS
115G UNSALTED BUTTER, CUT IN 2CM DICE
3 EGG WHITES
115G PLAIN FLOUR, SIFTED
1/2 TEASPOON VANILLA ESSENCE
1 TABLESPOON LEMON JUICE
1/4 TEASPOON MALDON SALT, GROUND FINE
BUTTER AND FLOUR FOR THE TRAYS

Blitz the sugar and lemon zest briefly in a food processor, processing until just combined, which should take about 30 seconds. Scrape down the sides and blitz for another 30 seconds. Scrape again, then add the butter and work until creamy – a few seconds. With the processor at full speed, add the egg whites through the feeder tube. Continuing to process, add the flour a spoonful at a time. When it is all incorporated, add the vanilla essence, lemon juice and salt, and work to a thick batter. Transfer to a mixing bowl and beat for a minute with a wooden spoon. Cover the top with cling film and leave to rest for 20 minutes.

Preheat the oven to 190°C. Butter two baking trays and dust lightly with flour. Drop heaped teaspoons of batter on the trays, trying to place 15–18 equidistantly on each tray and leaving the maximum amount of space between each blob to allow for spreading. Put both trays in the centre of the oven and bake for about 10 minutes or until the edges of the cookies start to brown. If you can't fit both trays on the same shelf, bake in two batches.

Transfer the cookies to a wire rack with a spatula to cool.

Pecan butter cookies

# Almond tuiles

Tuiles are pliant when hot, so when you set them over a mould, they retain that shape when they firm during cooling. This makes them ideal as edible containers or to fill like brandy snaps. They are also delicious, brittle enough to snap on the first bite, exploding in the mouth with a pleasingly chewy finish, almost like toffee.

**MAKES ABOUT 30 TUILES**

150G BLANCHED ALMONDS, SLIVERED OR CHOPPED
150G CASTER SUGAR
60G PLAIN FLOUR
1 EGG, SEPARATED + 1–2 EGG WHITES
40G UNSALTED BUTTER, MELTED

Preheat the oven to 180°C. Line a baking tray with a silicone mat or non-stick baking parchment.

In a bowl, mix together the almonds, sugar and flour. Add the egg yolk, stirring it in, then 2 of the egg whites to form a stiff batter that should fall thickly off the spoon. If too thick, add the remaining egg white, a little at a time. Stir in the melted butter.

Spoon 2 teaspoons of the mixture on to the baking tray and spread out into a 10cm circle using a fork dipped in cold water. Make another three circles on the tray, then bake for 5–10 minutes or until the edges of the biscuits have turned brown.

Immediately lift the biscuits off the tray with a fish slice or palette knife and drape over a long, thin rolling pin. The biscuits will harden almost at once into curved tuiles (roof-tile shapes), which you can then slide off. Alternatively, place the biscuits over upturned tumblers, pulling down the edges gently to produce cups. Continue baking and shaping the biscuits until all the mixture is used up.

# Parmesan biscuits

The ultimate, rich cheese biscuit, these make the perfect accompaniment to any aperitif and go particularly well with dry sherry. You can substitute a good mature farmhouse Cheddar for the Parmesan if you prefer.

**MAKES 40–50 BISCUITS**

335G PLAIN FLOUR
300G PARMESAN, FRESHLY GRATED
300G UNSALTED BUTTER, CHILLED AND DICED
$1/3$ TEASPOON CAYENNE PEPPER
$1^1/2$ TEASPOONS MALDON SALT, GROUND FINE
1 TEASPOON COARSELY GROUND BLACK PEPPER
1–2 TABLESPOONS COLD BOTTLED SPRING WATER

**TO FINISH**

1 EGG, LIGHTLY BEATEN
2 TABLESPOONS SESAME SEEDS
2 TABLESPOONS BLACK ONION SEED (NIGELLA)

Put the flour, freshly grated Parmesan and chilled diced butter in a food processor with the cayenne, salt and black pepper. Whiz to a crumb, then slowly add the cold water through the feeder tube until the dough forms into a ball.

Scrape out on to a lightly floured surface and roll into a cylinder. You will cut the biscuits from this, so size the roll accordingly. Cling-wrap tightly and refrigerate for at least 4 hours or overnight.

Brush the cylinder with beaten egg and roll in the mixed sesame and nigella seeds to coat all over. Wrap and chill for a further hour.

Preheat the oven to 180°C. Cut the cylinder into 5mm slices and lay these on non-stick baking trays, leaving at least 2cm space around them. Bake for 20–25 minutes or until golden brown. Transfer to a wire rack to cool.

# Meringues

Baker & Spice meringues are big – about 10cm across. People eat them on their own, sweet, crisp and as light as air.

Laurent Beauvois, who works in the shop, says they have always been a favourite with regular customers, particularly with children whose eyes light up at the sheer scale of the treat. "They are always a great conversation piece in the shop," he says. "People are surprised by the size and the intensity of the whiteness. They are literally the first display you see when you step through the door."

The difference in texture between our meringues and others comes from warming the egg whites and sugar over hot water before prolonged whisking, during which the meringue cools as it stiffens. Putting the meringues into a preheated oven at a slightly higher temperature than is usual and then turning the heat off and leaving them overnight is a way of introducing consistency in the product.

The professional baker always uses egg whites by weight. This is much more accurate than counting them.

**MAKES 12 MERINGUES**

115G EGG WHITES
225G CASTER SUGAR
30G FLAKED ALMONDS

Preheat the oven to 150°C. Cover 2 large baking trays with non-stick baking parchment or a silicone mat.

Put the egg whites and sugar in a bowl set over a pan of simmering water, and stir until the sugar has dissolved and the mixture is quite warm to the touch. Transfer the mixture to the metal bowl of a heavy-duty electric mixer and beat with the whisk attachment until thick and cool – about 15 minutes.

Spoon 6 large mounds of meringue on to each tray. Lightly sprinkle with the almonds. Place the trays in the oven, turn off the heat and leave the meringues to dry out overnight.

**Serve whole meringues with...**

... a fruit coulis

... vanilla or chocolate ice-cream

... whipped cream

... Greek yoghurt and seasonal berries

Or, toss berries with kirsch and sugar, mix with whipped cream and crushed meringues, and then freeze as a parfait. Or, ripple pieces of meringue through ice-cream by adding them in the last few minutes of churning.

# Pastries

A form of thin sheet pastry rather like filo was known in Roman times, and basic pastry in the form of virtually inedible food containers for pies was a feature of medieval cooking. In ever more sophisticated variations, pastry has been an essential part of a developed Western kitchen since the fifteenth century. In the 1420s an enterprising French cook incorporated butter into the folding and rolling process to create the first flaky pastry. Flaky remains to this day the finest example of the pastry cook's skill.

Today, pastry describes a multitude of different forms, from a basic shortcrust for tart shells – the 'short' referring to fat, as in the word shortening still used in America – through ever more buttery variations, to arrive at perfect puff pastry and, its ultimate and complex expression, the croissant. Pastry also includes hot water crusts – robust lard-based constructions for stand-alone pies – and choux, the least pastry-like pastry, a pipeable soft paste made elastic with eggs.

# MAKING PASTRY

The kitchen is not a laboratory, but comes closest to a scientific environment when we make pastry where precision is essential. With most cooking, we can make guesses based on experience. Pastry does not lend itself to such random modification, though everybody adapts and changes recipes. When these changes work, the minor adjustments they represent may be seen as incremental improvements, but do not look for revolutionary new methods. They do not exist. The first rule of pastry-making is to have an accurate set of scales and always to use them.

Pastry, particularly when cold butter is being added, does not react well to heat which is why in restaurants and bakeries the pastry making is kept as far away from the ovens as possible. You too should always work in as cool an environment as is feasible. A marble sheet for pastry-making is the perfect cold work surface, and this can be bought from kitchen shops. It is desirable but certainly not essential.

# Sweet pastry

This takes only seconds to make in a food processor, so it is a good idea to prepare two tart cases at the same time. One can be frozen, and then baked blind straight from the freezer without the necessity for a foil lining and weights, which means you can have a pastry case instantly to hand.

**MAKES 2 TART CASES OF 25CM DIAMETER**

500G PLAIN FLOUR

150G CASTER SUGAR

100G GROUND ALMONDS

380G UNSALTED BUTTER, CHILLED AND DICED
    INTO SMALL CUBES

1 EGG + 2 EGG YOLKS

1/2 TEASPOON GRATED LEMON ZEST

1 TEASPOON RUM OR BRANDY

PINCH OF MALDON SALT, GROUND FINE

Put the flour, sugar and almonds into a food processor and whiz at full speed for a few seconds. Add the butter dice and work again until just blended in. The mixture will resemble fine breadcrumbs. Add the whole egg and yolks, the lemon zest, rum or brandy and a minute pinch of salt, and work again briefly until the pastry balls.

Scrape out on to a sheet of cling film and either shape into a rough ball or roll into a cylinder about 5cm in diameter. Wrap and chill for at least 2 hours. Because of its high fat content this pastry can be kept in the fridge for a week, and it freezes well.

The amount of butter makes it difficult to roll out this pastry, so it is best to do this between two sheets of non-stick baking parchment. Divide the pastry in half. For each tart case, roll out one portion to a round about 5cm larger than the top of a 25cm detachable-based tart tin. Peel off the top sheet of parchment, then carefully pick the pastry up on the bottom sheet of parchment. Lay the pastry over the tin, paper side up, and gently peel off the paper as you lift and ease the pastry down the sides to fit, taking care not to leave any air between the pastry and the tin. If the pastry

has been rolled thin, fold the overhanging pastry back over to give a double thickness around the edges. Squeeze this between finger and thumb to amalgamate, making sure that the top of the pastry is just above the height of the sides of the tin, as the pastry will shrink back during cooking.

Alternatively, cut thin discs from the cylinder of pastry and overlap them slightly to cover the bottom and sides of the tart tin, pushing down to make a coherent shell. Take care to press into the corner where the sides and base meet so there is no air between the tin and the pastry. Make the edges slightly more solid than the base and push the pastry slightly above the sides of the tin.

To bake blind, preheat the oven to 190°C. Line the pastry case with a sheet of foil and fill with ceramic weights or dried beans. (The ceramic weights have the advantage of not making the foul smell dried beans do on re-use.) Bake for 15 minutes. Remove the foil and weights. Reduce the temperature to 150°C. Return the pastry case to the oven to bake for another 15 minutes for the base to finish cooking to a uniform pale golden-brown.

# Lemon tarts

The pâtissier's version of lemon tart uses a lot of butter and is therefore extremely rich. It is an elegant tart with a delicate but still lemony flavour.

**MAKES 10 INDIVIDUAL TARTS**

1 recipe SWEET PASTRY
(PAGE 131)
8 EGGS
35G CORNFLOUR
GRATED ZEST AND JUICE OF
4 LEMONS
235G CASTER SUGAR
225G UNSALTED BUTTER,
CUT INTO SMALL DICE

**DECORATION (OPTIONAL)**
GOOD-QUALITY BITTERSWEET
CHOCOLATE, MELTED

Preheat the oven to 170°C.

Roll out the pastry (or cut out discs) and use to line ten 8–10cm diameter fluted tart tins with detachable bases. Prick the pastry cases with a fork (there is no need for a foil lining and weights). Bake blind for 20 minutes or until set and pale golden brown. Set aside to cool.

Lightly whisk together the eggs and cornflour in a bowl.

Put the lemon zest and juice and the sugar in a large heavy-based saucepan and bring to the boil. Remove the pan from the heat. Whisk a little of the lemon-sugar mixture into the eggs, then whisk this mixture back into the remaining lemon mix in the pan. Return the pan to a low to medium heat and bring to a simmer. Cook for 1 minute, whisking constantly, then remove from the heat. Add the butter a few pieces at a time, whisking quickly after each addition. Transfer to a wide container. Cover the surface with cling film and leave to cool.

Put the lemon filling into a piping bag fitted with a 1.5cm plain tube. Pipe into the baked tart cases, swirling it up into a peak. If you like, decorate with a swirled drizzle of melted chocolate.

# Lemon curd tart

Lemon curd makes a very good tart and has the benefit of being pretty much foolproof in its preparation. The finish is quite sharp and those with a sweet tooth may want to add a further 60g of sugar to the curd mixture. Lemons tend to be wax-coated and, unless organic, will have been chemically treated, so always scrub them in soapy water, then rinse and dry before using.

**MAKES A 25CM TART**

8 EGGS
60G UNSALTED BUTTER
GRATED ZEST AND JUICE OF
6 LEMONS
225G CASTER SUGAR
25CM SWEET PASTRY TART CASE
(PAGE 131), BAKED BLIND

Whisk the eggs together in a bowl. In a heavy-based saucepan, melt the butter over a low heat. Add the eggs, lemon zest and juice and the sugar. Cook gently, stirring from time to time. When the mixture starts to thicken, stir constantly until a thick curd custard is formed.

Pour and spoon into the baked tart case and leave to cool and set before serving.

**Lemon tarts**

# Chocolate tart

Rich and dark, this tart is best eaten when the filling is warm but not hot. The better the chocolate, the better the tart.

**MAKES A 25CM TART**

220G BEST-QUALITY
BITTERSWEET CHOCOLATE,
CHOPPED
180G UNSALTED BUTTER
6 EGGS
280G CASTER SUGAR
85G PLAIN FLOUR, SIFTED
25CM SWEET PASTRY TART CASE
(PAGE 131), BAKED BLIND
ICING SUGAR FOR DUSTING

Put the chocolate into a bowl set over a pan of simmering water. The base of the bowl should not touch the water. Stir from time to time with a metal spoon until the chocolate has melted into a coherent mass.

Preheat the oven to 180°C.

Put the butter, eggs, caster sugar and sifted flour in the bowl of a heavy-duty electric mixer fitted with the whisk. Switch on at medium speed. Pour in the chocolate and beat for 10 minutes.

Put the baked tart case on a baking tray and fill with the chocolate mixture. Bake for 20 minutes. Transfer to a wire rack and leave to cool until warm.

Dust with icing sugar and serve with thick pouring cream.

# Chocolate and caramel tart

The flavours of chocolate and caramel contrast perfectly, balancing bitterness and sweetness on the tongue. The combination is rich and satisfying, nicely offset by the crisp crunch of the short pastry. The tart filling also makes the ultimate topping for shortbread bars (page 116): pour the caramel mixture over the baked shortbread in its tin and leave to cool and set. Finish with the chocolate topping, then refrigerate before cutting into neat bars.

**MAKES A 25CM TART**

225G CASTER SUGAR
100ML COLD BOTTLED SPRING
WATER
150ML SINGLE CREAM
115G UNSALTED BUTTER, CUT
INTO DICE
25CM SWEET PASTRY TART CASE
(PAGE 131), BAKED BLIND

**CHOCOLATE TOPPING**
170G GOOD-QUALITY
BITTERSWEET CHOCOLATE,
CHOPPED
30G UNSALTED BUTTER

Put the sugar and water in a heavy-based saucepan and bring to the boil. Lower the heat and use a thermometer to take the caramel to 180°C, when it will be a deep golden-brown. Remove the pan from the heat and gradually add the cream – start with a spoonful at a time because the mixture will foam up when the cold cream hits the incandescent toffee. When all the cream has been incorporated, gradually stir in the butter to give a smooth, creamy sauce. Pour into the baked tart case and leave to set.

Put the chocolate in a bowl set over barely simmering water. When melted, remove from the heat and beat in the butter. Spread over the set caramel using a plastic spatula, then swirl the surface attractively with a skewer. Leave to cool completely before serving.

Chocolate and caramel tart

# Butter puff pastry

Puff is the ultimate pastry, a really rich, multi-layered and extravagantly buttery construction. Correctly made, it is so light one is not aware of its weight in the hand or its high fat content on the tongue. This is the supreme product of the pastry cook's alchemy: flaky, with each layer as thin, crisp and fragile as the next, the whole made extraordinary by the air that separates them.

The skill in making puff pastry is to interleave the butter and air into the flour as it forms a dough by rolling, turning and chilling, but while doing so to be as economical in the working as possible, to prevent over-working of the gluten in the flour. The consequence of too much rolling and stretching is elasticity. That is what you

want in a bread dough, but in pastry it results in it shrinking back unacceptably. The chilling is also vital. If the butter softens it will become oily and seep through the flour, giving a greasy surface to the pastry layers and causing them to stick together, so inhibiting the rise.

Making puff pastry is not easy, although perhaps more time consuming than really difficult. But, of course, like anything technique-based, it gets better with repetition. It is best prepared a day ahead. The Baker & Spice technique of making a beurre manié, or butter paste, of flour and butter is different from most recipes which interleave chilled butter into the pastry. It produces an excellent, buttery, flaky puff.

5

## Butter paste

340g unsalted butter, softened
150g French T550 flour or plain flour

## Assembly

560g French T550 flour, or 280g plain flour and 280g strong bread flour + extra for sprinkling
4 egg yolks
180ml bottled spring water
2 teaspoons Maldon salt, ground fine

Make the butter paste: put the butter and flour in the bowl of a heavy-duty electric mixer fitted with the paddle. Mix on the slowest speed until combined. Remove to a sheet of cling film and shape into a rectangle about 6mm thick. Wrap in the film and keep in a cool place (not in the refrigerator) while you make the dough.

For the assembly, put the flour, egg yolks, water and salt in a bowl and mix to a dough. If necessary, add another teaspoon or two of water, but be careful – the dough will soften on resting. What you want is a smooth but fairly tight dough. Remove to a lightly floured surface and knead for 10 minutes or until very smooth and elastic. Shape into a ball, wrap in cling film and leave to rest for 1 hour or, ideally, overnight.

Lightly flour the work surface and roll out the dough into a rough square about 8mm thick. Place the rectangle of butter paste in the centre and fold the corners of the dough over the top to cover the paste completely (1, 2). Wrap in cling film and refrigerate for 30 minutes.

Place the dough on the lightly floured surface. Roll the dough out, rolling away from you, into a long rectangle about 65–70 x 35–40cm and 1cm thick (3, 4). Fold one end in by a sixth and then the other end in by a sixth (5). Fold both ends over again by a sixth so that they meet in the centre (6). Now fold the two together, as if you are closing a book (7).

Next turn the dough so the fold is to one side. Roll it out gently away from you again into a long rectangle about the same length as before. Fold one end of the dough in by a third (8) and then the other end in by a third, over the top of the first third. This is a single turn.

Spread a sheet of cling film over a tray, place the dough on top and cover tightly with cling film. Leave in the refrigerator or a cool place for 1 hour.

Set the dough on the floured work surface so the fold is to one side. Roll out into a rectangle again and give it a single turn, followed immediately by another single turn. Wrap in cling film and leave in the refrigerator overnight before using.

## On pastry

"Good ingredients are the foundation for excellent pastry making. Take the finest you can find – the butter from your table, good dark chocolate, the cream you would serve with the ripest strawberries – and search for the right flour, soft and unbleached. Never, ever economise on flour (one of the least expensive ingredients you will use) as its quality will enhance the flavour of everything you mix with it. Try to work in the morning, when the kitchen is cooler, and be methodical, weighing and mixing with a swift and careful hand.

"Pastry making is a skill that really does improve with repetition. You learn about getting it perfect by doing it over and over. Enjoy your work. Allow it to become a pleasure, and it will soon feel effortless. Remember that the best pastry is defined by the indulgence it encourages." DAN LEPARD, BAKER

# Cheese straws

Traditional cheese straws are dense and very rich. Good-quality puff pastry provides an effortless opportunity to create a much lighter variation on the theme. These are delicious, yet quick and easy to make.

Include different spices with the cheese, giving a prickle of heat with chilli flakes or taking this one step further by scattering on finely shredded fresh chillies. Add paprika for a smoky contrast or shredded spring onions or shallots to cut the richness of the cheese. Alternatively, Dijon mustard could be spread thinly on the pastry before adding the cheese. For a different effect, instead of sprinkling sesame seeds on top, substitute onion seeds or cumin seeds.

**MAKES 20–25 STRAWS**

400G BUTTER PUFF PASTRY
(PAGE 136)
85G PARMESAN OR FARMHOUSE
CHEDDAR, FRESHLY GRATED
BLACK PEPPER
1 TABLESPOON SESAME
SEEDS (OPTIONAL)

**GLAZE**
1 EGG YOLK
1 TABLESPOON MILK

Preheat the oven to 180°C. Line two baking trays with non-stick baking parchment.

Roll out the pastry into a neat rectangle about 4mm thick. Distribute the grated cheese evenly on half the pastry and grind black pepper over all. Fold the other half of the pastry over, pressing down gently. Cut across in 5mm strips, then, holding the ends, twist each strip to make a spiral shape.

Beat the egg yolk and milk together in a bowl. Brush the cheese straws with the glaze and shake the sesame seeds over, if liked. Lay the straws on the baking trays.

Bake for 20–25 minutes or until puffed and golden brown. Remove to a rack and cool before serving.

Tarte fine aux pommes and Chestnut mille feuilles

# Chestnut mille feuilles

Mille feuilles – literally thousand leaves – is nothing more than three slices of baked puff pastry layered in a triple-decker sandwich with whipped cream and fruit or, as here, with a rich chestnut cream. The success of everything you do with puff pastry is determined by its quality. You could make a very pretty-looking mille feuilles with shop-bought puff pastry made from oil or a commercial solid margarine, but you would not want to eat it. Butter puff is essential.

It is suggested that you weight the pastry during baking with a wire rack, if you have one that will fit in the oven. This compensates for any unevenness in the rolling which can result in an uneven rise. The rack does not stop the pastry rising, but it does ensure a flat surface. It is not, however, essential.

**SERVES 8**

400G BUTTER PUFF PASTRY
(PAGE 136)
150G CHESTNUTS IN SYRUP,
DRAINED
2 TABLESPOONS SIFTED ICING
SUGAR + EXTRA FOR
DUSTING
1 VANILLA POD
300ML DOUBLE CREAM

**PASTRY CREAM**
50G CASTER SUGAR
2 EGG YOLKS
25G CORNFLOUR
1 VANILLA POD
250ML MILK
25G UNSALTED BUTTER

First make the pastry cream. Whisk the sugar, egg yolks and cornflour together in a bowl. Split open the vanilla pod over a plate and scrape out the seeds. Put both the pod and seeds into a heavy-based saucepan with the milk and slowly bring to the boil. Remove from the heat and whisk a third of the hot milk into the egg mix. Quickly tip the egg mix into the milk pan, scraping any remaining egg from the sides of the bowl, and immediately whisk together. Return the pan to the heat and bring back to the boil, stirring constantly. Boil for 1 minute. Pass through a sieve into a bowl, discarding the vanilla seeds in the sieve (wash and dry the pod for making vanilla sugar). Add the butter and stir until melted. When the pastry cream has cooled to warm, cover the surface with cling film and leave to cool completely.

Preheat the oven to 180°C. Line a baking tray with non-stick baking parchment or a silicone mat.

Roll out the puff pastry on a flour-dusted surface to a 30cm square about 5mm thick. Lay the pastry square on the baking tray. Put a wire cooling rack on top of the pastry. Bake for 25–30 minutes or until the pastry is crisp and brown. Carefully turn the baking tray over so that the pastry rests on the wire rack, then leave to cool in a warm dry place.

Put the drained chestnuts in a food processor and pulse-chop briefly to a rough paste. Add 300ml of the pastry cream (any left over can be used as a tart or éclair filling, or topped with fruit for a simple pudding). Sweeten with about 1 tablespoon of icing sugar, or to taste. Split the vanilla pod and scrape the seeds into the mixture. Fold together, then cover and chill for 20–30 minutes.

Lightly whip the cream with the remaining tablespoon of icing sugar to soft peaks. Fold one-third of the cream through the chestnut mixture.

Carefully transfer the pastry square to a work surface. Trim the edges with a sharp knife, then cut into three equal strips. (Alternatively, if you prefer to make individual mille feuilles, cut the pastry into 24 even-sized rectangles.)

Spread one strip of pastry with the chestnut custard, then lay a second strip on top. Spread the remaining whipped cream over this and finish with the final layer of pastry. With a palette knife remove any excess filling from the pastry, and dust the top of the mille feuilles with icing sugar. For a decorative finish, score lines in the sugar with a hot skewer.

# Pithiviers

**The pithiviers is a classic of French pâtisserie. Make and bake it ahead of time – though it isn't complicated, you need to give yourself time and space to work in a cool kitchen, when the house is quiet and you can concentrate on perfecting the finish.**

**SERVES 8–10**

500G BUTTER PUFF PASTRY
(PAGE 136)

**ALMOND CREAM**
250G GROUND ALMONDS
250G CASTER SUGAR
250G UNSALTED BUTTER,
SOFTENED
2 EGGS
50G PLAIN FLOUR

**GLAZE**
2 EGG YOLKS
1 TABLESPOON MILK

Make the almond cream: place the almonds, sugar and butter in a food processor, and blend until smooth and the butter is thoroughly incorporated. Add the eggs and flour, and blend again for a moment to combine. Transfer the mixture to a 20cm springform cake tin lined with cling film and spread evenly. Cover and chill until firm.

Divide the puff pastry into two pieces, two-thirds and one-third. Roll out the smaller piece of dough into a rough circle about 25cm diameter and 6mm thick. Place on a small baking tray lined with non-stick baking parchment or a silicone mat.

For the glaze, lightly beat the egg yolks with the milk.

Take the almond cream out of the refrigerator and turn out of the tin. Centre it on the circle of pastry. Brush around the exposed pastry edge with the egg yolk wash. Roll out the remaining larger piece of pastry to a circle 6mm thick and lay it carefully over the almond filling. Starting at the centre, begin to press and smooth the pastry out, sealing it close to the almond cream and the base circle of pastry. Be careful not to capture any air bubbles underneath the pastry. If you do, lightly prick them with a pin. Now seal around the edges with a fork, pressing firmly down to seal the two circles together.

Take a round bowl or dish that will enclose the filled part of the shaped pastry snugly inside. Press the bowl firmly down over the top so that the edge of the bowl indents lightly into the pastry edge. Remove the bowl, then cover the pithiviers with cling film and refrigerate for 1 hour.

Brush the surface of the pithiviers with the egg yolk wash. Let this dry for 5–10 minutes. Now take a small sharp knife and trim round the edge of the pastry, leaving a 3cm border. Cut a scalloped edge on the border, if you like. Very lightly score through the domed top of the pastry, drawing curved lines that radiate out from the centre to the bottom of the dome. Finally, cut a small hole in the centre of the dome, so that any air created as the pithiviers bakes will be released. Refrigerate, uncovered, until the oven is at temperature.

Preheat the oven to 180°C.

Remove the pithiviers from the refrigerator and bake for 15 minutes, then reduce the oven temperature to 150°C and continue to bake for 35–40 minutes or until risen and golden brown and a skewer inserted through the hole in the centre comes out clean. Carefully transfer the cooked pastry to a wire rack and leave to cool.

Serve warm with a little lightly whipped double cream.

Plum tart

# Plum tart

To be exceptional this tart is wholly dependent on the quality of the pastry used. Those who choose not to attempt to make their own puff pastry are in good company, and you can now buy good frozen butter puff pastry (puff pastry made with vegetable oil or lard is only acceptable in savoury dishes).

Frangipane is the pretty French word for almond paste. We make ours with hazelnuts and almonds.

**MAKES A 25CM TART**

12 SLIGHTLY UNDER-RIPE
VICTORIA PLUMS
225G BUTTER PUFF PASTRY
(PAGE 136)
4 TABLESPOONS APRICOT JAM
BUTTER FOR THE TIN

**HAZELNUT FRANGIPANE**
200G UNSALTED BUTTER,
SOFTENED
150G CASTER SUGAR
125G GROUND ALMONDS
125G GROUND HAZELNUTS
100G PLAIN FLOUR
3 EGGS

Make the frangipane: in the bowl of a heavy-duty electric mixer fitted with the whisk, beat the butter with the sugar at high speed until light and fluffy – about 8 minutes. Add the ground nuts and flour, and beat briefly. Add the eggs, one at a time, whisking to combine. Reserve.

Cut the plums in half, discarding the stones, then cut each half in half and reserve.

Preheat the oven to 190°C. Brush a 25cm detachable-based round tart tin with melted butter.

Roll out the pastry into a thin circle. Using a rolling pin, transfer the pastry into the tin and press in gently to line the bottom and sides. Fold the edges over to give thicker sides to the pastry case, then roll gently but firmly over the top of the tin with the rolling pin to cut through the pastry and give a neat rim.

Spread the hazelnut frangipane in the pastry case, then set the plum quarters into the frangipane so that they stand upright – that is, cut faces vertical. Bake for 15 minutes, then reduce the oven temperature to 150°C and bake for a further 35–40 minutes, when the frangipane will have risen up around the plums and set. Remove from the oven to a rack and cool a little before lifting the tart out of the tin. Warm the jam in a small pan until melted. Press it through a sieve to remove any large pieces of fruit, then brush over the warm tart to glaze.

# Tarte fine aux pommes

This is an absolutely classic tart. We dust the apples with a spoonful of sugar just before the tarts go in the oven and then add more gloss with a jam glaze after baking.

**MAKES 4 INDIVIDUAL TARTS**

400G BUTTER PUFF PASTRY
(PAGE 136)
4 TABLESPOONS PASTRY CREAM
(SEE CHESTNUT MILLE
FEUILLES, PAGE 141)
4 GRANNY SMITH APPLES
1 TABLESPOON SUGAR
2 TABLESPOONS APRICOT JAM

**GLAZE**
1 EGG YOLK
1 TABLESPOON MILK

Preheat the oven to 200°C. Line a baking tray with non-stick baking parchment or a silicone mat. Divide the pastry into four and roll out each portion into a thin circle about 15cm in diameter. Place on the baking tray. Scrape the pastry cream over the pastry with a palette knife to coat thinly.

Cut the apples in quarters and remove the cores, but leave the skins on. Slice the quarters in paper-thin slices and fan these on the pastry discs, with each new slice slightly overlapping the last. Leave a 1cm rim of pastry uncovered. Lightly beat the egg yolk with the milk, and brush this glaze over the pastry rim. Sprinkle the apples with the sugar.

Bake for 15 minutes, then lower the oven temperature to 150°C and bake for a further 5 minutes. The apples will have taken on a golden glaze while the pastry will have puffed up round the rim. Warm the jam in a small pan until melted. Press it through a sieve to remove any large pieces of fruit, then brush over the warm tarts.

# Pear tarte renversée

For a tarte Tatin, peeled and segmented apples are baked in caramel with a pastry lid on top; this becomes the base when the cooked tart is inverted for serving. When such a tart is made with any other fruit, such as the pears here, it should properly be called a tarte renversée, which means upside-down tart. The buttery caramel and fruit juices soak into the pastry when the tart is turned upside down, so it should be served warm to be at its best, though not straight from the oven when people could burn themselves with the super-heated caramel.

Cooks develop their own little tricks to ensure a perfect result. At Baker & Spice we make the caramel first, then pour it into the mould and leave it to cool. The pears cook slowly as the caramel melts and mixes with the fruit juices, making it less likely that the caramel will burn. Use pears that are just ripe but still firm.

**MAKES A 23CM TART**

7–8 COMICE PEARS
JUICE OF 1/2 LEMON
500G BUTTER PUFF PASTRY
(PAGE 136)

**CARAMEL**
250G CASTER SUGAR
150G UNSALTED BUTTER
50ML BOTTLED SPRING WATER

Make the caramel: in a saucepan over a low to medium heat, warm the sugar, butter and water, stirring to dissolve the sugar, then bring to the boil. Reduce the heat and cook until you have a dark caramel, on the reddish side of brown. Carefully pour the caramel into a 23cm cake tin and tilt to cover the bottom evenly. Leave to cool while you prepare the fruit.

Preheat the oven to 190°C.

Peel the pears, cut in half and remove the core. Put the halves in a bowl and toss with the lemon juice to prevent discoloration.

Roll out the pastry to about the thickness of a pound coin. Using a plate 27–28cm in diameter as a guide, cut out a circle. Fold the circle of pastry in half and then fold again to make a quarter. Arrange the pear halves in the tin, cut side up, packing them closely together in a fan shape and filling all gaps. Lay the folded pastry over one quarter of the tin and unfold to cover the fruit, tucking the edges of the pastry inside the rim of the tin.

Bake for 35–40 minutes or until the pastry is well risen and golden brown. Remove from the oven to a wire rack and leave to cool for 5–10 minutes.

Cover the top of the tin with a large flat plate, leaving a small gap at one side. Tilt to pour off any excess caramelly juices into a bowl; reserve these. Then, holding the plate and tin firmly together, invert the two. Sit the plate on a flat surface and lift the tin away from the tart. Cut in wedges and serve warm with whipped cream and the reserved caramelly juices.

# Croissants

For 200 years croissants, which originated in Vienna in the familiar crescent shape, were made from enriched bread dough. The delightfully buttery yet feather-light puff pastry and yeast croissant, which has become the definitive statement of a pastry cook's skill, is a comparatively recent French development, occurring perhaps 100 years ago. Making croissants is time-consuming and takes practice to get right, but since it is now difficult to buy a fine croissant even in France, there is every reason to try. This is a much simpler method than most, yet it produces an excellent, flaky result.

Croissants are at their best when still warm from the oven. Their high butter content means that they freeze well and will not start to deteriorate in the freezer for at least 2 weeks. Before eating, they should be put frozen into a 250°C oven for 5 minutes, then removed to a rack and left to stand for 5 minutes. Raw unproved croissants also freeze well, as does any uncooked pastry. Raw croissants should be thawed in the refrigerator overnight, then put to rise, covered, until doubled in size before baking.

**MAKES 16 CROISSANTS**

1 SACHET FAST-ACTION YEAST
500G STRONG WHITE FLOUR +
EXTRA FOR SPRINKLING
110ML WARM BOTTLED SPRING
WATER (20°C)
110ML COLD MILK (10°C)
20G MALDON SALT, GROUND FINE
70G CASTER SUGAR
250G UNSALTED BUTTER

**GLAZE**
1 EGG YOLK
1 TABLESPOON MILK

Make a sponge: in a bowl whisk together the yeast, 100g of the flour and the warm water. Cover the bowl with cling film and leave in a warm place for 2 hours or until the sponge has risen by at least one-third and is clearly active, with lots of bubbles.

Put the remaining flour, the milk, salt and sugar in the bowl of a heavy-duty electric mixer and add the sponge. Switch on at the lowest speed and work with the dough hook for 2 minutes. Turn up the speed slightly and work for 6 minutes, when the dough will be soft and sticky and coming away from the sides of the bowl. Put the dough in a polythene bag and leave overnight in the refrigerator.

The next day put a sheet of cling film on the table and dredge with flour. Lay the butter, which should be firm but not hard from the fridge, on top. (If too soft you will not be able to control it.) Sprinkle a little flour on to the butter and, with a rolling pin, knock it out into a rectangle about 1cm thick. Wrap with the cling film and place it in a cool part of the kitchen. (If the room is hot, return the butter to the refrigerator for a few minutes.)

Take the dough out of the bag and put it on a floured work surface. Knock back with the rolling pin. Scatter more flour on top of the dough and on the rolling pin, then roll out, turning frequently, into a rectangle about 1cm thick. Brush off any obvious flour, then put the unwrapped butter in the centre. Fold the edges of the dough over the butter so that they slightly overlap at the top and the butter is completely enclosed.

Scatter some more flour over. Rolling always away from you, roll the dough out into a long rectangle about 67 x 40cm. Fold one end in by a sixth and then the other end in by a sixth. Fold both ends over again by a sixth so that they meet in the centre. Now fold the two together, as if you are closing a book. Turn the dough so the fold is to one side. Roll it out gently away from you again into a long rectangle about the same size as before. Fold one end of the dough in by a quarter and then the other end in by a quarter so that they meet in the middle. Now fold the two together, as if you are closing a book. Seal the edges with pressure from the rolling pin. Wrap in cling film and refrigerate for 30 minutes to 1 hour.

Make a triangular template 17.5 x 17.5 x 15cm from card or rigid plastic. Roll the dough out

on the floured surface to as neat a rectangle as you can, about 75cm long, 30cm across and 4mm thick. Trim to give straight edges, then cut into two pieces lengthways. Using the template, mark out and cut 8 triangles from each piece of dough.

Lay the triangles, one at a time, on the lightly floured surface with the narrow point away from you. Roll up away from you, finishing with the point in the middle and underneath. Lay the croissants on large baking trays lined with non-stick baking parchment, leaving space round them to allow for expansion. Cover with cling film and leave in a warm place to rise until doubled in size, which should take 1–2 hours.

Preheat the oven to 200°C.

For the glaze, whisk the egg yolk and milk together. Brush lightly on to the croissants, brushing from the middle outwards so the glaze does not get between the dough layers – this could cause them to stick and would impair the uniform rise. Bake in two batches in the centre of the oven for 10 minutes, when they will have expanded and started to colour. Reduce the oven temperature to 150°C and bake for a further 20–25 minutes or until risen and golden brown. Cool on a wire rack, arranging the croissants so they are not touching.

# Danish pastries

We use croissant dough for our Danish pastries because it gives a crisper and less doughy finish. The pastry can be cut into squares or rounds and baked in tins, or it can be shaped into coiled ropes. Pastry cream and fruit are traditional toppings. The baked pastries are glazed here with apricot jam, but you could also use a lemon icing (see Lemon cake, page 107).

**MAKES 6 PASTRIES**

300G CROISSANT DOUGH
(PAGE 148)
A SELECTION OF FRESH, CANNED
OR BOTTLED FRUIT, SUCH AS
PEACHES OR NECTARINES,
PLUMS, APRICOTS, APPLES,
PEARS, FIGS OR PASSION
FRUIT FLESH, OR READY-TO-
EAT DRIED FRUIT, SUCH AS
RAISINS, FIGS, CHERRIES,
APRICOTS AND CANDIED PEEL
ABOUT 150G PASTRY CREAM (SEE
CHESTNUT MILLE FEUILLES,
PAGE 141)
LIGHT SOFT BROWN SUGAR FOR
SPRINKLING (OPTIONAL)
FLOUR FOR ROLLING
3–4 TABLESPOONS APRICOT JAM
CORN OR SUNFLOWER OIL FOR
THE TINS

**GLAZE**
1 EGG YOLK
1 TABLESPOON MILK

If baking the pastries in tins, put six 8–9cm fluted tart tins on a baking tray and brush each inside lightly with oil.

On a floured work surface, roll the dough to 6–7mm thickness. Using a 10cm round cutter (or a sharp knife), cut discs or squares from the dough and lay these in the tart tins. Press the dough lightly into the corners of the tins. Alternatively, shape the dough into thin ropes and coil round into 8cm circles on baking trays lined with non-stick baking parchment or a silicone mat. (At this point you can freeze the shaped dough for up to 1 week; thaw before rising.) Cover with cling film and leave in a warm place to rise until doubled in size, which should take 1–2 hours.

Preheat the oven to 180°C.

If using fresh or preserved fruit, cut it into neat slices or dice, peeling as necessary. Dried fruit should be soaked briefly in hot water and then dried on a towel, unless it is very plump and moist.

For the glaze, whisk the egg yolk and milk together. Spoon 1–2 tablespoons of pastry cream into the centre of each dough case, and spread the cream with the back of the spoon to cover the bottom evenly. Arrange the fruit on the pastry cream, fanning slices neatly or scattering on diced or small fruit. Sprinkle with brown sugar, if liked. Brush the exposed edges of the pastry case with the egg wash.

Bake for 35–45 minutes or until the pastry is risen and golden brown.

Warm the jam in a small pan until melted. Press it through a sieve to remove any large pieces of fruit, then brush over the warm pastries to glaze.

Danish pastries and
Pains au raisin, ready
for baking

# Pain au raisin

Pain au raisin is really a grown-up sticky bun, the dried fruit plumped in rum, the surface attractively glazed. Interestingly, during an experimental sub-contracted delivery programme at Baker & Spice, it was always the boxes of pain au raisin that became mysteriously depleted somewhere between the bakery and the customers, giving credence to the phrase, 'they are simply irresistible'.

**MAKES 6 PASTRIES**

300G CROISSANT DOUGH
(PAGE 148)
250G RAISINS OR SULTANAS,
SOAKED IN WARM WATER
FOR 30 MINUTES
1 TABLESPOON CASTER SUGAR
1/2 TABLESPOON RUM
FLOUR FOR ROLLING
3 TABLESPOONS APRICOT JAM

**GLAZE**
1 EGG YOLK
1 TABLESPOON MILK

Line a baking tray with non-stick baking parchment or a silicone mat.

On a lightly floured surface roll out the dough to a 6–7mm thick rectangle.

Drain the soaked fruit and put it in a bowl. Add the sugar and rum and toss to coat. Spread evenly over the surface of the dough. Take one long edge of the dough rectangle and roll up like a Swiss roll, taking care none of the fruit falls out. With a sharp knife, cut this cylinder into slices 2–3cm thick. Place them on the lined tray, with space around them. (They can now be frozen for up to a week; thaw before rising.) Cover with cling film and leave in a warm place to rise until doubled in size, which should take 1–2 hours.

Preheat the oven to 180°C.

For the glaze, whisk the egg yolk and milk together. Brush this over the pastries. Bake for 35–45 minutes or until risen and golden brown.

Warm the jam in a small pan until melted. Press it through a sieve to remove any large pieces of fruit, then brush over the warm pastries to glaze.

# Choux paste

Choux is a pastry oddity, being part cooked prior to baking and – with its high egg and water content – presenting as a pipeable paste. During baking the water in the paste creates steam internally, encouraging the choux to expand rapidly and set as a crisp shell with a hollow centre. This space can be filled with set custards, whipped cream or savoury mixtures.

Accurate measurement of the ingredients is important, though in this recipe the precise amount of egg is deliberately not specified. You need about one egg to each 30g of flour, but eggs vary in size and flours have different absorption levels. The thing to do is beat in 3 eggs sequentially and then beat in the fourth a little at a time, stopping when the mixture holds to a spoon and only drops from it slowly. If you don't put in sufficient egg, the paste will be too dry to expand; if you add too much the mix will be too sloppy to pipe.

150G PLAIN FLOUR
3–4 EGGS
100G UNSALTED BUTTER
1 TEASPOON MALDON SALT, GROUND FINE
250ML COLD BOTTLED SPRING WATER

Sift the flour into a bowl. Have 3 eggs to hand, whisking the fourth to a liquid in a bowl and reserving.

Put the butter, salt and water in a heavy-based pan and bring to the boil over a medium heat. As the water comes to the boil, remove from the heat and dump in the flour in one go. Immediately stir briskly with a wooden spoon until the flour and liquid are evenly combined.

Lower the heat and return the pan over it, beating continuously for a minute, when you will have a coherent mass that comes away easily from the side of the pan. Remove from the heat and leave to cool for about 3 minutes. (If you add the eggs

immediately the mixture may cook them, setting curds and ruining the mixture.)

Beat the first 3 eggs into the mixture, one at a time, making sure each egg is completely incorporated before adding the next. The mixture should be smooth and glossy. If too stiff, trickle in some of the beaten fourth egg from the bowl, beating well, and continue adding egg until the pastry looks and feels right.

Leave to cool to room temperature, then use immediately. If left too long the choux paste will stiffen so that you will not be able to pipe it or spread it easily.

# Mexican hats

The pastry puffs and lifts off the baking sheet as it bakes, forming an unusual shape. We call them Mexican hats as they appear extravagantly brimmed, like a sombrero. Pairs of the crisp, airy discs can be filled with lightly whipped double cream or pastry cream (see Chestnut mille feuilles, page 141), perfect with seasonal berries.

**MAKES 15 PAIRS OF CHOUX HATS**

1 RECIPE CHOUX PASTE
(SEE OPPOSITE)
ICING SUGAR FOR DUSTING
BUTTER FOR THE BAKING TRAY

Preheat the oven to 180°C. Take the largest heavy baking tray that will fit in your refrigerator and in the oven, making sure that it is spotlessly clean, and rub the tray all over generously with soft butter. Refrigerate it for about 20 minutes.

Put the choux paste on the work surface next to the tray. Put a spoonful of paste on the tray and spread it with a palette knife or rubber spatula, starting at one edge, to make a rough circle about 10cm across and 4–5mm thick (1). Don't worry if it is a little uneven. The ripples made by the spatula will produce a more interesting hat. With your finger trace a neat circle in the paste, cutting cleanly through to the tray (2). Wipe any excess paste from your fingers. Spread another circle of paste on the tray, about 2cm from the first, and repeat until you have filled the tray.

Place the tray on the middle shelf of the oven and bake for 15 minutes, then reduce the temperature to 160°C and bake for a further 10–15 minutes or until the hats are puffed, lightly browned and crisp. Lift the hats on to a rack to cool (3). Discard the choux trimmings left on the tray.

Sandwich the choux hats together in pairs with the chosen filling, and dust with icing sugar before serving.

# Éclairs

Of all the choux paste creations, éclairs are perhaps the best known and most widely enjoyed. With their crisp, light and neutral-tasting shell, the contrastingly rich filling and the shiny fondant icing on top, éclairs deliver a great deal for very little effort. They are easy to pipe, though it is a good idea to heat the knife or scissors you use to cut the paste as it extrudes so the cut is clean and the sticky paste does not adhere to the blade. When the pastries come from the oven it is important to puncture them immediately, so internal steam does not soften the case. To be enjoyed at their best, they should be eaten as soon after they are filled and iced as possible.

If you have more fondant icing than you need for the éclairs, it will keep well in the fridge in a covered container.

**MAKES 12–14 ÉCLAIRS**

1 RECIPE CHOUX PASTE (PAGE 152)
PASTRY CREAM (SEE CHESTNUT MILLE FEUILLES, PAGE 141) OR WHIPPED CREAM FOR FILLING
BUTTER FOR THE BAKING TRAY

**FONDANT ICING**
225G CASTER SUGAR
75ML BOTTLED SPRING WATER
2 TEASPOONS LIQUID GLUCOSE
OPTIONAL FLAVOURING:
FOR CHOCOLATE, 15G GOOD-QUALITY BITTERSWEET CHOCOLATE, GRATED, OR COCOA POWDER TO TASTE;
FOR COFFEE, 1/2 TABLESPOON STRONG ESPRESSO OR COFFEE ESSENCE
CORN OR SUNFLOWER OIL FOR THE SLAB

First make the fondant icing: put the sugar and water in a pan over a low heat and stir to dissolve the sugar. Add 1/2 teaspoon of the glucose (or a pinch of cream of tartar), then increase the heat and bring rapidly to the boil. Boil to the soft ball stage (115°C on a sugar thermometer). Pour on to a lightly oiled marble slab and leave to cool for 3–4 minutes. (If you proceed while the sugar is too hot, the icing will go grainy.) Working with a palette knife or metal scraper, scrape under the mass, repeatedly scooping it up and over itself in a figure-of-eight movement. Continue working like this for about 10 minutes or until the mass becomes opaque and too stiff to lift with the knife. Then start kneading with your hands, pressing and folding until the icing is smooth and pliable. Form into a ball, wrap in cling film and refrigerate for at least 24 hours before using.

Preheat the oven to 200°C. Butter a baking tray and chill in the refrigerator. Put a sharp knife or scissors in a jug and pour boiling water in to cover the blade.

Put the choux paste in a large piping bag fitted with a 2cm plain tube. Squeeze the bag down and twist the top until the first sign of paste extrudes, then pipe out on the baking tray in 10cm lengths, cutting them with the hot knife or scissors. Leave space between the éclairs to allow for expansion.

Place the tray on the middle shelf of the oven and bake for 15 minutes, when the éclairs will be well risen and have started to colour. Reduce the oven temperature to 160°C and bake for a further 10–15 minutes or until the éclairs are lightly browned and crisp. Remove, immediately slit open to allow any remaining steam to escape and transfer to a wire rack to cool.

Soften the fondant in a bowl set over simmering water. As it starts to soften, add the remaining liquid glucose. If flavouring the icing, add the chocolate, cocoa powder, espresso or coffee essence while the fondant is being melted. Remove from the heat and continue stirring until the icing coats the back of the spoon. The consistency should be like that of double cream.

Fill the éclairs with pastry cream or whipped cream, piping it into the slit. Hold each éclair upright over the bowl of fondant and spoon the icing on the top side, letting it run down to make an even layer. Leave to cool and set before serving.

**Mexican hats and Éclairs**

# GLOSSARY

**active yeast** Commercially produced yeast either in cultured or reconstituted dried forms. Also called brewers' yeast and brewers' sugar fungus, it is made up of the living cells of the yeast strain *Saccharomyces cerevisiae*. When fresh, it is usually sold in small, moist, compressed cakes.

**allspice** Aromatic brown berry the size of a large peppercorn that is dried in the same way. In its complex aroma one can smell hints of mace, cinnamon and cloves.

**baguette** Light (250g), long (75cm) French loaf baked with soft white flour (T550) which originated in Paris as late as 1920. It is characterised by a beautifully thick, crackling-crisp crust, but stales within hours.

**baking powder** Complete raising agent, a mixture of bicarbonate of soda and acid salts, that only needs moisture to activate it. Baking powder also contains a larger percentage of ground starch, which is included to absorb moisture from the air and prevent premature activation in the tin. It is used in conjunction with soft flour to make 'quick' breads.

**banetton** Linen-lined wicker basket, of different shapes and sizes, in which doughs are proved.

**barm** Raising agent containing yeasts from the froth produced during beer fermentation.

**beignet** Deep-fried, yeasted bread dough. The name is interpreted differently in different parts of the world – it can be a plain doughnut or a fruit fritter.

**beurre manié** Paste made from equal amounts of flour and butter.

**bicarbonate of soda** Raising agent, more properly sodium acid bicarbonate. When bicarbonate of soda, an alkali, is mixed with an acid, a chemical reaction is kick-started and carbon dioxide is given off.

**biga** Italian version of poolish, based on the high-protein '00' flour used for pasta.

**bolting, boulting** Successive sieving of flour to make whiter, refined flour.

**bran** Outer husk of wheat.

**brioche** Sweet yeasted bread enriched with butter and egg.

**Callibaut Couverture** Fine high-cocoa-content chocolate with a strong bittersweet taste.

**choux (pastry)** Pipeable, egg and flour paste used for making hollow cases such as éclairs and profiteroles.

**cinnamon** Dried inner bark of a tropical tree. Cinnamon is preferable bought as rolls or quills of bark rather than as a ground powder, because the latter rapidly loses flavour and aroma.

**crème fraîche** Rich cream with a distinctive tangy taste. It is made from double cream mixed with buttermilk heated to a constant 75°C for several hours until it thickens and stabilises.

**crumpet** Round, yeast-raised unsweetened bread. Crumpets are cooked as a batter in ring moulds on a griddle, which produces a dark brown base and a pale top pocked with holes.

**deflate** Pressing raised dough to expel the carbon dioxide trapped as bubbles by the gluten during proving.

**éclair** Long choux container usually filled with whipped cream or pastry cream.

**ferment, fermentation** Process during which carbon dioxide is given off. This is a result of yeasts producing alcohol as a byproduct of getting chemical energy from sugars.

**ficelle** White loaf made as a baguette in length, but only 125g in weight so consequently much thinner.

**focaccia** Rectangular yeasted white bread with a dimpled surface. The bread is dressed liberally with olive oil and sea salt just before it goes in the oven. It often has rosemary leaves on top, too.

**fougasse** Oval Provençale yeasted flat bread distinguished by slashed holes cut through the loaf in a rough herringbone or leaf-on-the-branch pattern. It may be plain or filled.

**gluten** Combination of two proteins found in wheat grain which, when moistened, bind together, creating thin, elastic strands. These form membranes that trap the gas, causing the dough to rise.

**granary flour** Wholemeal flour with a variety of seeds.

**grissini** Crisp bread sticks first made in Turin.

**hard flour** White wheat flour with protein levels of between 10 and 14%.

**knead** Working and mixing flour and water together to make a coherent, elastic and pliable mass (dough). Kneading can either be done by hand or using an electric mixer fitted with a dough hook. The process encourages the gluten in flour to stretch, expand and acquire the necessary elastic and plastic properties to trap gas bubbles given off during yeast fermentation (leavening, proving).

**knock back** Aggressive technique to deflate dough after initial proving(s).

**lemon zest** Thin outermost layer of the rind. Zest is used in many recipes as it contains the volatile oils that deliver the most intensely lemon flavour. Unless organic, always scrub lemons thoroughly before removing the zest because of chemicals and the coating of antifungal wax, the latter retarding oxidisation.

**levain, leaven** Dough colonised by airborne yeasts, which is used to raise sourdough breads.

**mace** See nutmeg.

**meal** Coarse flour.

**miche** Large, round French country loaf, usually a sourdough.

**mille feuilles** Multi-layered puff pastry confection. Literally 'thousand leaves', this is not an accurate description as there are really 723.

**muffin** Small, sweet 'quick' bread raised with bicarbonate of soda or baking powder.

**muscovado** Dark brown sugar produced as the first stage of refining from boiled sugar cane. It has an intense, treacly flavour. Muscovado is a Portuguese word meaning unrefined.

**nutmeg** Seed of the fruit of *Myristica fragrans*, the tropical nutmeg tree, which originated in the Moluccas but is today cultivated in many tropical countries. The seed is covered with a reddish, fibrous membrane that separates it from the flesh of the fruit. When dried and flattened this membrane becomes mace. Mace and nutmeg smell and taste similar and are interchangeable, though mace is stronger in flavour.

**oats** Coarse cereal popular with horses and eaten by humans in porridge, muesli and oat cakes.

**organic** A word that implies something is free of chemicals or other additives and has been grown or raised in a chemical-free environment.

**palmier** Sugary biscuit made from puff pastry.

**pane bianco** Classic Italian loaf baked with minor regional variations throughout Italy – their version of a French pain de campagne.

**pastry cream** Thick, flour-stabilised egg custard usually flavoured with vanilla. It is an essential preparation in pastry making, being used to fill tarts and many other pastries.

**peel** Flat beech-wood head attached to a long shaft, used for loading and unloading breads from traditional ovens.

**pithiviers** Glazed, round puff pastry pie with a rich, sweet filling. Pithiviers is traditionally scored on the top in radiating curved lines.

**polenta** Meal ground from dried field corn (maize).

**poolish** Starter batter colonised by airborne yeasts, which is used to raise sourdough breads.

**pretzel** Loosely twisted knot of crisp white yeasted dough. The history of the pretzel can be traced back to Roman times, but they are today seen as American as the first pretzel factory was established in Pennsylvania in 1861.

**profiterole** Small choux bun that may be filled with either sweet or savoury creams.

**prove** Resting kneaded dough in a warm place during which time it rises.

**quick bread** Bread raised using chemical raising agents, such as cornbread, soda bread, muffins and scones.

**rye** Low-gluten cereal. When milled it produces a dark, heavy flour with a pronounced flavour.

**semolina** Durum wheat that is more coarsely ground than standard wheat flours.

**soda bread** Soft wheat flour loaf usually raised with bicarbonate of soda; originally Irish.

**soft flour** White wheat flour with a protein content of between 6 and 10%.

**sourdough** Bread leavened using wild yeasts and given a distinctive sour tang from the lengthy fermentation involved.

**sponge** Preliminary flour, yeast and water batter. Once active, the sponge is used to raise the subsequent dough.

**spring water** Purified bottled still water without chemicals.

**sumak** Red powder made from the dried berries of the shrub of the same name, which is used extensively in Iraqi cooking.

***taux des cendres*** French designation of the level of bran in a flour, based on the ash left behind after the flour has been incinerated in a laboratory at 900°C.

**vanilla pod** Dried long, thin pod of the orchid *Vanilla planifolia*. The principal flavour resides in the seeds.

***Viennoiserie*** French pâtisserie term for fine flaky pastries such as puff pastry and croissants, in which crisp layers result from the careful incorporation of butter during repeated rolling and chilling.

**wheat germ** Oily embryo of the wheat 'berry' or kernel. Wheat germ is a concentrated source of proteins, vitamins and minerals.

**wholemeal, whole wheat** Flours darker in colour because they are made using elements of the whole wheat berry including some of the wheat germ and bran.

**yeast** Microscopic single-cell organism that produces alcohol and carbon dioxide as it grows, a process called fermentation. To do this it needs sugars, moisture and warmth.

**zatar** Mixture of equal amounts of powdered sumak and dried ground marjoram and thyme.

# INDEX

# ACKNOWLEDGMENTS

**54-56 Elizabeth Street**
**Belgravia**
**London SW1W 9PB**
**Tel:** 020 7730 3033
**Fax:** 020 7730 3188

**47 Denyer Street**
**Chelsea**
**London SW3 2LX**
**Tel:** 020 7589 4734
**Fax:** 020 7823 9148

**20 Clifton Road**
**Maida Vale**
**London W9 1SU**
**Tel:** 020 7266 1122
**Fax:** 020 7266 3535

**75 Salusbury Road**
**Queen's Park**
**London NW6 6NH**
**Tel:** 020 7604 3636
**Fax:** 020 7604 3646

**www.bakerandspice.com**

We have about 65 full-time staff working to create the food we make every day. Of course, this cast changes from time to time, but without the extreme hard work and dedication of our exceptional crew we would not be where we are today. The staff who have helped to create the shops we have today, listed chronologically, are:

**For the bakery:** David Frequelin, Remi Georgelin, DL, Amir Allon, Martin Aspinwall, Jason Warwick, Remek Sanetra, Henri Bellon de Chassy, Damon Cowan, Sally Parsons, Amar Slimani.

**For the Viennoiserie:** Patrick Lozach, Ram Sivaram, Martin Doak, Lionel Rocher, Ilan Schwartz, Mariangela Pratt.

**For the pâtisserie:** Henri Berthaud, Yannick, Amal Ibrahim, Ari Aboso, Alexandra Queruel, Yvan Cahour, Dorit Mainzer, Jeanne Hertz, Linda Osedo, Louise Riviere, Jaime Foa, Megan Jones, Mark Lazenby, Markus Herz, James Webb.

**For the traiteur:** Lorraine Dunne, Sammy Leopold Santos, DL, Michelle Wong, Kate Lewis, Sami Tamimi, Ruth Taylor Hunt, Pavel Kuzdak, Cayetano Lopez.

**For the shop:** Karen Copland, Natalie Laurent, Zoe Field, Tamsin Borlase, Anne Boyle, Fiona Kinnear, Stephane Boucton, Leonor Gomez, Laurent Beauvois, Helena Allon, Fabio Calascibetta, Alessandra Figini, Belen Mateo, Jaclyn Dove, Emma O'Reilly, Naima Ali, Anna Plym, Jenny Mellquist, Andrea Novak, Eric Ackermann, Daniel Marcolin, David Doulay, Candice Nieper, Kirsty McGregor, Amanda Hale, Anna-Marie Briers, Ari Economakis.

**Kitchen assistants:** Vince Mejia, Tito Bosales, Cesar Aristizabal.

**For the bread factory and gail force:** Amnon Mer, Pierre Corneille, Richard Vintiner, Samantha Oyez, Jackie Hobbs, Terry Stockwell, Nimal Kandihi.

**Our drivers:** David Ormston, Paul Stimson, Steve Bragg, Richard Fenton, Ray Mechell, Errol Palmer, Arthur Albert.

**Our friends:** Melanie Pini and Sophie Braimbridge (who suggested and created our first series of chef demonstrations), Naomi Kaplan (forever a source of inspiration), Anissa Helou, Peter Gordon, Jeremy Lee, Lyn Hall, Ursula Ferrigno, Giorgio Locatelli, Elizabeth Luard, Alastair Little, Juliet Peston, Heston Blumenthal, Jonathan Archer, John Kelly, Enzo Zaccharini, Honor Chapman, Sarah Standing, and the customers who have supported us from the beginning.

**All our recipes have an origin,** as do the recipes in every cookbook. Though these recipes have been written or adapted and tested by Dan Lepard and Richard Whittington especially for this book, the ingredients, techniques and inspiration have come to us from our friends. Additional recipe credits are:
Dorit Mainzer for the Chocolate pecan cake, Devil's food cake, Marble cake, Lemon cake, Parmesan biscuits and Chocolate chip cookies.
Naomi Kaplan for the Plum cake and Pecan butter cookies.
Jason Warwick for the basic levain and Roquefort and walnut fougasse.

**For the production of this book,** Baker & Spice would like to thank Divertimenti of Fulham, Kitchen Aid UK, Phillip Brittain and Solstice, Neal's Yard Dairy, Jeni Wright, Peter Howard, Coralie Bickford-Smith, Bridget Bodoano and Caroline Perkins.

We would like to thank Emily Andersen for the use of her photographs on pages 7, 9, 10, 13, 14, 19, 20/21, 31, 35, 45, 49, 91, 93, 94/95, 102, 114/115, 129 and 138.